W9-CGS-021

BOLD SCHOOL

BOLD SCHOOL

An Inquiry Model to Transform Teaching

Tina Jagdeo & Lara Jensen

PORTAGE & MAIN PRESS

© 2016 by Tina Jagdeo & Lara Jensen

Excerpts from this publication may be reproduced under licence from Access Copyright, or with the express written permission of Portage & Main Press, or as permitted by law.

All rights are otherwise reserved, and no part of this publication may be reproduced, stored in a retrieval system, or transmitted in any form or by any means – electronic, mechanical, photocopying, scanning, recording, or otherwise – except as specifically authorized.

Portage & Main Press gratefully acknowledges the financial support of the Province of Manitoba through the Department of Culture, Heritage & Tourism and the Manitoba Book Publishing Tax Credit, and the Government of Canada through the Canada Book Fund (CBF) for our publishing activities.

Gall-Peters projection map on page 63 – Mike Linksvayer/ Wikimedia Commons/ CC-BY-SA-3.0
Mercator Projection map on Page 63 – © Portage & Main Press

Printed and bound in Canada by Friesens
Cover and interior design by Relish New Brand Experience

LIBRARY AND ARCHIVES CANADA CATALOGUING IN PUBLICATION

Jagdeo, Tina, 1970-, author
        Bold school : an inquiry model to transform teaching /
Tina Jagdeo, Lara Jensen.

Includes bibliographical references.
ISBN 978-1-55379-672-5 (paperback)

        1. Inquiry-based learning. I. Jensen, Lara, author
II. Title.

LB1027.23.J34 2016   371.39   C2016-901979-9

PORTAGE & MAIN PRESS

100-318 McDermot Avenue
Winnipeg, MB, Canada
R3A 0A2
Tel: 204-987-3500
Toll free: 1-800-667-9673
Toll-free fax: 1-866-734-8477
Email: books@portageandmainpress.com
www.portageandmainpress.com

For Ingrid Jagdeo and Queen Eileen

CONTENTS

INTRODUCTION

W E'VE OFTEN JOKED ABOUT HOW A CONVERSATION WITH OPRAH WOULD PLAY OUT.

"So, Tina and Lara," Oprah would ask, "why do you want all schools to be bold?"

"Well, Oprah, the school experience should feel like real life, not just preparation for the next grade. We want students to think deeply and know everyone has a voice that can affect change. In Bold Schools, there is an urgent need to create a community of learners who collaborate on common goals to make a difference in the lives of our students and others in our community."

Both of us are passionate about teaching and learning; we love to investigate new strategies to make schoolwork feel worthy of everyone's time. Over the past 15 years, we have had the opportunity to work with exemplary educators who know what "good" looks like in the teaching and learning department. We talked to these educators to capture what exactly happens in their individual classrooms to make students feel engaged, excited, and like inquirers in these Bold Schools.

We call this book *Bold School* to share how teaching and learning can transform classrooms. What is a Bold School? Bold Schools embrace education that is student-centred, concept-based, and incorporate new learning to make an impact on our world. These schools haven't completely done away with "old school" subjects and teaching practices that work. Some of the underlying principles that unite Bold Schools are their use of inquiry-based learning and teaching to give students multiple opportunities to think critically, creatively, and compassionately about real issues, as well as design change projects to make a difference.

We feel that the time is right to make these Bold School changes to teaching and learning; recent brain research has highlighted the importance of experimentation, trying new things, and learning from mistakes — all an integral part of learning through inquiry.

Technology is also transforming the landscape of education and the world so significantly some are comparing its impact as akin to the changes precipitated by the Industrial Revolution. Ten years ago, who knew we would be able to use a pocket-sized computer to easily access and share images or information with anyone, anywhere, anytime? For the first time in history, teachers and students have access to the same information not so long ago only teachers possessed. Students can now access information on almost any subject with a few taps on a screen. With so much information widely available and easily accessible, teachers and textbooks are no longer the font of knowledge in the classroom. Students have more opportunity for self-directed learning, and we can shift our focus in schools from the memorization of many facts to learning critical, compassionate, and creative thinking.

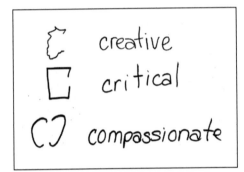

Students suggested icons to represent critical, creative, and compassionate thinking. They thought an angular C should represent the research involved with critical thinking, a wavy C should represent creativity, and two Cs in the shape of a heart should illustrate compassion.

As Albert Einstein said, "Education is not the learning of facts, but the training of the mind to think." This cannot be done if we focus solely on rote learning and the memorization of facts.

Through critical thinking, real questions are asked and problems are researched from multiple perspectives to support local and global communities. Creative thinking is the development of original, outside-the-box ideas. This process benefits from collaboration with others to address a range of issues. Compassionate thinking represents thinking from the heart. Working together, teachers and students think deeply about how to use new knowledge to devise plans and projects to contribute to individual, local, or global well-being. With these three modes of thinking, we focus on teaching lifelong skills, and see inquiry in action.

In Bold Schools...

We teach through ideas. The focus is on big ideas, rather than on tasks or activities. In doing so, students deepen their understanding. Ideally, once students learn about a new idea, they produce and communicate their new knowledge in many forms. The drama and excitement of education intersect when you find a concept or an abstract idea that can be unpacked to gain a better understanding of a real-world issue. For example, the big idea of deforestation illustrates the concept of balance. Once students start to work with multiple concepts, learning unfolds.

power	humility	conflict
change	energy	harmony
tempo	balance	dynamics

Above are concepts that can be explored in a variety of subjects.

Students and teachers grapple with real-world issues. During the inquiry process, students conduct research to answer their questions, but the ultimate goal of an inquiry-based classroom is to develop enduring understanding. For example, habitat loss and desertification are issues closely connected to unregulated deforestation practices. Teachers might share videos and pictures of logged areas around the world to start discussions about land use and responsible logging practices. Building curiosity and interest in the issues is key for teachers. As a result of teacher-led provocations, class discussions, and consolidated knowledge, students have a desire to develop creative solutions to problems. The hope is that by studying real-world issues students will want to make a difference in the world on many levels – in their classroom, their school, their community, and globally.

We collaborate to find creative solutions to challenging problems. Humans are social, so the classroom is not silent. We learn from and support one another, including student-student, student-teacher, and teacher-teacher interactions. Students work in small groups to gather information, share their current understanding or ideas, develop theories, and solve problems. When we work together others challenge our thinking, and we develop a deeper understanding of the issues than we would have on our own.

Students contribute to curriculum. The contributions of students, especially their wonderings and prior knowledge, are valued as connection points for learning. They might choose when certain activities happen, which skills need to be practised, or what new information needs to be gathered. Students might select the resources they use to investigate the impact of logging with support from classroom teachers, librarians, technology, and learning-strategies educators.

Use learning to create change. Connecting to local community issues can help students connect their passion to an issue to make a change. If students have learned a lot about an issue and want to embark on a change project, it feels significant when they can share their learning with an audience who actually wants or needs the work students do. Having an authentic audience provides motivation for producing good-quality work that is "worthy of the world" (Maiers 2015). Students might

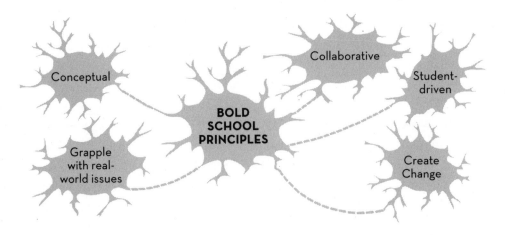

The Bold School is one where all of these elements coexist to create local and global well-being.

decide to create an event at school to share their learning, or they may organize a planting event for their school community that demonstrates their understanding of the impact of deforestation. In our school, after a unit investigating this concept, grade 5 students contacted an organization called LEAF to stage a tree-planting event for members of the school community. They pitched this idea to the school's Eco-Warriors committee, and on Earth Day, the planting event took place. Students from older grades carried the water buckets and shovelled deep holes for younger students to fill with saplings. Everyone worked together to make sure all the bulbs and trees were appropriately covered and watered. Working on a change project allows students to demonstrate an understanding of issues beyond recording their knowledge through a pencil-and-paper test. For students, these types of projects are the ones they remember many years after traditional schooling has ceased.

Why Bother?

We feel the Bold School approach can benefit students:

› When we teach through concepts and big ideas, students transfer their learning from one context or subject to another.

› When students collaborate with others, whether they are in their class or on the other side of the world, they are able to learn from those who have more experience or have a different perspective. They learn new ways of looking at things and have more ideas on which to build.

› When students play a role in driving the learning process in the classroom, they feel valued and that their opinions and ideas matter. They take ownership of the skills and knowledge acquired and are more engaged.

› When we teach about issues and try to make a difference in our lives or in the lives of others, students see the connections between what they are learning in school and the real world. Helping others leads to a feeling of satisfaction and accomplishment. Because issues are based in the real world, students can develop compassion as they learn from or about real people. If efforts are made to address real-world issues, then students learn to think creatively to solve problems.

> When students share their learning, they are empowered to make decisions and see the outcomes or consequences of their actions.

When teachers use the same approaches in their work with one another that we advocate for students, teachers are also able to learn from one another, examine the issues in their schools, and affect change in their spheres of influence. The Bold School approach can also benefit teachers and the school community:

> When we teach through concepts and big ideas, we collaborate to make connections between subject areas and save time in the classroom by not reteaching what students have already learned in other classes.

> When we work to understand the underlying causes of problems or challenges within the school and consider multiple options for moving forward, we use an inquiry approach, which we can then model for students and learn about challenges students may face as they use it.

> When we share our challenges, mistakes, and solutions with others, we are able to learn from one another and build on each other's ideas.

> When we observe students and differentiate instruction based on what we see, or invite students to help determine what to do next, we are better able to meet their learning needs and increase engagement.

If we are preparing students for jobs that might not have been created yet, then we need to be targeted in our approach to teaching and learning. While teaching through inquiry takes time to plan and do and requires a lot of collaboration (i.e., time for meetings, difficult conversations, coordination, miscommunication), the benefits outweigh the challenges.

How this Book Is Organized

You can start small and progressively implement Bold School strategies in your own classroom. In this book, we propose a possible framework for a Bold School. We will start at the classroom level. As the chapters progress, we will layer in more elements you can add to increase your level of "boldness." One teacher in one classroom is the base model of inquiry. However, "no man is an island" – this base model can also be scaled to include more than one classroom. Once you have a base in place, you have the opportunity to include more people and resources, including digital, to support learning through inquiry in your classroom. We believe changes made with one teacher can start an entire school on a journey to boldness.

> Chapter 1: We provide an overview of the Bold School principles and a framework for planning and implementation.

> Chapter 2: We explore current brain research and how sharing some of the fundamentals of how the brain works can enhance ongoing learning, risk taking, and making mistakes in an inquiry classroom.

> Chapter 3: We explain ways to shift teaching from topics to concepts.

> Chapter 4: We explore ideas or provocations to kickstart units as we observe and get to know issues.

> Chapter 5: We explore strategies for asking effective questions and developing a research practice.

> Chapter 6: We discuss ways to deepen inquiry by adding more support teachers, technology, and small-group work to investigations. Teachers can join with other teachers, students, administrators, parents, outside experts, and partner schools to promote Bold School thinking and learning.

> Chapter 7: We flex our empathy muscles and try to determine how we can use new learning to affect our own lives or the lives of others in our local or global community.

> Chapter 8: We explore different types of change projects students can undertake to spark action.

> Chapter 9: We focus on the role administrators play to support Bold School principles throughout the learning community. Inquiry is not always linear, so we need to develop sustainable school systems and administrator support to teach through this model.

In each chapter, we share ideas for assessment and reflection and some of the challenges teachers might face teaching through inquiry. With teaching and learning, it seems likes nothing is ever finished, which causes us to always reflect and make revisions to our approach based on new thinking. The "Oh Snap" sections address some of the mistakes and difficulties we have encountered and document some of our learning from these mistakes.

Each chapter will provide real-life classroom examples, challenges you might face, and possible solutions. We view the solutions as recipes from which you can pick and choose. We fully recognize these solutions are not applicable in all situations and hope you will take them and tweak them to work in your context.

"So, Oprah, it is not easy to teach in this way. But if we work in collaborative teaching teams with the support of administration, and listen to our collective wisdom as teachers, we hope to see teaching through a Bold School method occur in more classrooms. This method values what each student brings to the educational process and provides students with thinking skills that will endure in spite of inevitable change."

1 / BOLD SCHOOLS VALUE THINKING PROCESSES

Over the years, we have explored many models to see how other educators approach teaching and learning. The common element in much of their work is the desire to give students explicit strategies to think. With the increase in information computers provide, it appears as if our society is becoming more and more an economy of thinking. Given that we do not know for what types of jobs or careers we are preparing our students, thinking is the most important skill to teach, because it is universal and timeless in an age of change.

Building thinking skills is our goal. We want to help students to think critically, creatively, and compassionately. Inquiry is the process that allows us to teach these thinking skills. When you teach through inquiry, you provide students with multiple opportunities to think about real issues and to design change projects to make a difference.

The process we propose drives inquiry in the classroom in a manageable way. Students and teachers can start to deepen their knowledge and understanding of a problem or issue using the following four questions. These questions help to structure thinking, planning, and teaching.

OUR INQUIRY PROCESS QUESTIONS

1. How can we observe and get to know an issue?

2. How can we tease out the facets of the problem or issue?

3. How might we use what we have learned to contribute to our lives or the lives of others?

4. What type of change project can we design for a real audience?

Standing on the Shoulders of Giants

A number of educational, creativity, inquiry, and change experts have shaped our understanding about effective ways to teach and learn. We owe much of our thinking on how to begin to plan curriculum to Grant Wiggins and Jay McTighe (1999). Their emphasis on starting with the end in mind and thinking about the enduring concepts you want your students to understand keep our units focused on big ideas on which to hang skills and knowledge and give them context. H. Lynn Erickson (2006) has also been pivotal in our understanding of the timeless and universal benefit of teaching through concepts. Her work shows us the value in wrapping content from any subject around conceptual thinking as a way to make learning more meaningful and connected to the real world.

When we think of the students, we agree wholeheartedly with Adam Cox (2008), Angela Maiers (2015), and Alan November (2012b) who know children crave significant projects that allow them to make and be the change in the world. Marc Prensky (2010) advances this argument when he talks about the expertise students can bring to the class. As teachers we need to leverage and build on the open mindset many of our students possess about creating and producing digital content and work together with them to make a difference in their own lives or the lives of others.

Stephanie Harvey and Harvey Daniels (2009) have provided us with so many gifts. At first, we were drawn to their emphasis on the explicit teaching of literacy and research skills to support inquiry. Their four-step inquiry process expands the role of the student in inquiry and encourages students to dig into an issue with the end goal of sharing their learning. We have tried to build on their work to expand teaching through inquiry beyond subjects that are literacy and research based. Our model of inquiry, like theirs, hinges on strong research practices and students sharing their learning with others.

Teri Burgess (2015), Susan Elliott and Stan Kozak (2014), and Marc and Craig Kielburger have taught us the importance and effect of students working on change projects. Burgess made us think about the multiple ways students can take action beyond the realm of fundraising. She shares strategies like awareness campaigns, designing prototypes, and event planning that students can use to get the word out about a particular issue. Elliott and Kozak provide us with many environmental examples of action projects students have developed through a process of inquiry. Marc and Craig Kielburger's "Me to We" (2014) curriculum and service trips provide many examples of what change can look like locally and globally. "Me to We" challenges schools to engage in several local and global action projects each year.

In terms of assessing and evaluating student work, Dylan William and Paul Black (2005), Anne Davies (2000), and Damian Cooper (2006) have all stressed the importance of providing formative assessment or feedback to students in the moment. This has shaped the organizational work we have done in setting up small groups whenever possible. Debriefing after a chunk of learning highlights the importance of checking in with students to see where they are, what they know, and what we need to plan next to move their thinking forward. Formative feedback has helped us stay in the moment with the students and to learn alongside them.

Our model of inquiry and thinking differs from and builds on the work of the experts we have consulted in several ways:

> Students play a bigger role in the planning process. We want student thinking and questions to inspire inquiry whenever possible. This way, students remain engaged in the process, and we benefit from having more thinkers and contributors in the room.

> We advocate that students conduct change projects to act on their learning and experience civic engagement. Going beyond fundraising ensures students actively participate in sharing their learning. We want students to link their learning to local and global issues.

› We use divergent thinking to build empathy once learning about a particular issue is consolidated. Although these key concepts of empathy and action are embedded in many global curriculum documents, we wonder if there is enough explicit support built into everyday teaching to help students engage in projects to make a difference. Empathy is woven throughout our inquiry process, driving student questions and investigation. We explore multiple audiences to determine who can benefit from our knowledge and new understanding. Then, our model explicitly supports student action based on their learning and provides a process for teachers to scaffold. Conducting change projects to help others represents the culmination of critical, creative, and compassionate thinking.

The example below explains how the team of grade 2 teachers at our school (home room, librarian, and learning-strategies teachers) and students used the Inquiry Process Questions as they began to explore the role of humour in our lives.

Students giggling at the start of their new unit exploring the concept of humour.

How Can We Observe and Get to Know the Issue?

What It Is

Inquiry always starts with an issue to explore or a problem to solve. Teachers often begin to plan an inquiry with a review of their curriculum documents and then determine how best to get students to care about issues. Teachers can kickstart student thinking by inspiring students to bring their observations and questions about the world to the classroom. This is an opportunity for teachers to find books or artifacts, for example, to promote discussion about an issue. During this phase, a community of learners can engage many of their senses to help understand the world. Learners can read about current events in newspapers or other nonfiction sources and watch documentaries with family and friends to gain information. Issues to explore might emerge from the curriculum, real-life scenario witnessed at school, events that happened in the local community, or in the life of a student or teacher. During this stage, students begin to develop knowledge and understanding to determine potential directions to explore.

Why It Is Important for Inquiry

Before students can ask meaningful questions about an issue, they need to know something about the content they are studying. Having these discussions will start the critical-thinking faculties flowing as students start to flex their inquiring minds.

What It Looks Like in the Classroom

The classroom teacher and teacher-librarian selected joke books, humorous poetry, newspapers, and picture books for students to become familiar with different forms of humour. Students chose any text they wanted and curled up to read during DEAR time or after they finished assigned work. They also viewed videos and cartoons that showcased examples of humour from different parts of the world. The classroom teacher designed a survey, so students could interview other adults in the school about what they found funny. The teacher's role in this phase of the inquiry was to collaborate with the teacher-librarian to locate resources and to design experiences to foster curiosity about the unit.

How Can We Tease Out the Facets of the Problem or Issue?

What It Is

This step involves determining which questions you need to research to get to the crux of an issue to unravel its complexity. Students ask questions and explore issues of interest to deepen understanding. To do this, you need to know what makes a good question and what resources are available to answer it. Crafting deep questions helps teachers and students delve into the bigger issues. We often need to revisit questions and sometimes alter them based on results from research. This can be an iterative process. This stage requires students to dig in: read, talk to experts, test hypotheses, and conduct group experiments to clarify thinking. Teachers work together with students during this process to try to figure out the connections across disciplines, determine the different perspectives at play for a particular issue, and question why students now believe their conclusions are correct. Critical thinking helps students to look at issues from multiple points of view before developing their own point of view. Creative thinking helps teachers and students combine ideas to develop provocative questions and use a flexible approach to accessing information.

Why It Is Important for Inquiry

The process we describe drives inquiry: the questions students and teachers ask lead to research, learning, unlearning (debunking myths), and relearning.

What It Looks Like in the Classroom

Guided-reading lessons focused on comprehension strategies, but the texts were selected to delve into the function of humour in people's lives. During the small-group sessions, students discussed poems written by Shel Silverstein and Jack Prelutsky to figure out how poetry can affect people's mood. In their role as guide, teachers ensured students were working in their zone of proximal development and provided explicit skill instruction when necessary. After each guided-reading lesson, all students were invited to share some of their new insights during debrief time.

Teachers pushed student thinking on a topic by asking open-ended questions. For example, "Do you use humour to diffuse an argument with friends?" The teachers shifted into co-learner mode, learning alongside students and modelling the learning process. Questions to which the group genuinely wanted to know the answers, such as, "Who cracked the first joke in history?", "When did humour first start?", and "Can you grow up and become a humorologist?", helped to get at the role humour can play in our lives.

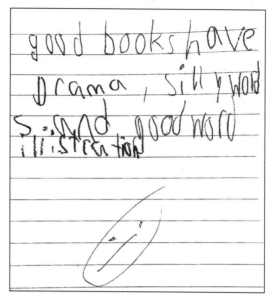

Students listen to a teacher read a story aloud and document their criteria for a humorous book.

How Might We Use What We Have Learned to Contribute to Our Lives or the Lives of Others?

What It Is

This phase is the time for the classroom community to consider what has been learned so far and how what they have learned might be used to make a difference in their lives or in the lives of others. Asking students questions such as, What can you do with the knowledge you have gained? Is there anyone else who could benefit from what you have learned? engages students in compassionate or "heart thinking." Ideally, at this point, students will identify with those affected by the issue. Through the creative-thinking process, students brainstorm and imagine possibilities for contributing to the lives of others. This process should not be rushed, or key options might not be explored.

After reading about Patch Adams, students brainstormed how they might use their learning to help others.

Why It Is Important for Inquiry

This stage of learning is important because students are brainstorming and using divergent thinking skills to figure out how to use their knowledge to help others. This is when students engage critical, creative, and compassionate thinking skills.

What It Looks Like in the Classroom

A guided-reading session about Patch Adams, the physician who used humour to bring moments of levity to children in hospitals, sparked the idea of raising funds to support a clowning program at a local hospital. A student suggested raising money by hosting a Funny and Yummy Bake Sale to sell treats and student-created books. At this juncture in the inquiry, the students collaborated with one another to generate a host of logistical and informational questions such as, How can we actually find and fund a clowning program? What is involved in making a donation to a hospital? Could we hold a bake sale? Could we sell the humour books to the community?

What Type of Change Project Can We Design for a Real Audience?

What It Is

Now you are designing and implementing change projects with your students. Every student needs a job that matters, with each role part of a greater whole. This is the time to test prototypes, create awareness campaigns, start a letter-writing campaign to a member of government, or plan events. At this stage, make sure all the resources required to take action successfully are available.

Why It Is Important for Inquiry

Students engage their convergent thinking skills to determine and implement an action to make a difference to their lives or the lives of others. Students, through real-life experiences, feel firsthand what it is like to make a difference in their own lives, locally and/or globally.

What It Looks Like in the Classroom

Teachers and students worked together to plan the bake sale and create the humour books. In this phase of the inquiry, the teacher, in a combined role as guide and co-learner, helped students develop a plan of action. The class determined when to hold the sale, who to invite, and where it should be held. Teachers wrote notes in the agenda to request that parents and students bake together and to bring in the treats on the appointed date. The teacher worked with small groups to edit, publish, and price humour books before the sale day. It was a thrill for the students, when bake-sale day arrived, to share their books and baking. Students who never seemed to care about the presentation of their work suddenly realized the importance of clarity and legibility, knowing that a real audience would be viewing their bake-sale signs and published books. The unit ended with another debrief discussion to get feedback on the event, to reflect on key learning, and to pose new questions to drive future inquiries. Maybe next year the students will want to host a junior "Just for Laughs" festival as a new change project.

Assessment and Reflection Ideas

Ongoing assessment and reflection are built into each stage of the inquiry process. Teachers make time during the process to conduct inquiry debriefs for the class to reflect on past learning and new learning. Should something be done differently next time? The grade 2 students wondered if it might be fun to have a cupcake-only sale.

Should they invite some visitors from the clowning program to attend? They wanted to determine if there were any new issues that needed addressing. One of the students suggested that comedians come to visit their class as a way to kick off the unit. This made the grade 2 teacher think of inviting a member of staff who had training in comedy in for a visit the following year. Teachers and students always need to think about what they have done and if it worked. If certain aspects of the unit did not work, indicate that new plans need to be devised.

The Role of the Teacher

The role of the teacher in a Bold School has shifted and expanded to support inquiry. The teacher as mentor feels like a familiar role; we are used to sharing our knowledge and discipline expertise with students. A less familiar role is that of teacher as co-learner: embracing the idea that there are many teachers, and that teachers can learn alongside students. Now, both teachers' and students' questions can shape the work in the classroom. As a result, student ideas can significantly affect instruction and ways to demonstrate learning.

Borrowing from athletics, teachers now act as academic coaches, too. This role highlights the importance of teachers providing ongoing feedback to inform student learning rather than providing the bulk of feedback at the end of a process after summative work is submitted.

Teachers can wear a number of hats at different stages of the inquiry process. As a teacher, adopting a flexible, open stance to curriculum planning and execution often means allowing students to play a bigger role in the learning process. These different roles are discussed below.

Teacher as Mentor

Be an observer. The challenge for teachers in an inquiry-based classroom is to observe the verbal and nonverbal messages at play in the classroom and look for what sparks students' curiosity. As students work in small groups, the teacher can move from group to group to probe student thinking and guide them as they help one another co-construct knowledge or create solutions to problems. Associate teacher Christine Cochrane observed that the weather was changing in the fall and invited her students to collect fallen leaves to start a Discovery Centre. While collecting in the garden, the students noticed a fallen sunflower and asked to take it back to the classroom. The students started to percolate with questions about their new discovery. "The seeds are so small and the sunflower is so big. Does the size of the seed matter?" The teacher began to document their wonderings on sticky notes and posted them at the Discovery Centre. Making student thinking visible serves many purposes. It can acknowledge the validity of student questions, give students a jumping-off point to build on one another's questions, and help teachers gain insight into students' current understandings.

Design exploratory moments. In addition to documenting student conversations, Cochrane chose materials like clay, crayons, scrap paper, soil, small containers, mini shovels, magnifying glasses, blocks, Lego, and literature for students to investigate,

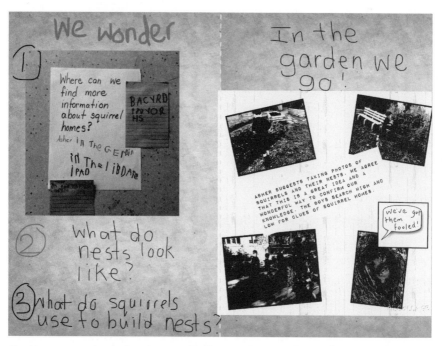

Cochrane conceived of and created a discovery centre for students to post their questions and test their hypotheses.

and the discoveries began. For example, out of the blocks, Johnny constructed flowers and shared that he had planted flowers in his own garden. By reading available books and using scrap paper and crayons, another student made an informational booklet on how to plant a seed.

As teachers, we notice what captures students' attention and connect their curiosity to the curriculum. Cochrane thought of ways to help students understand the needs of plants and to conduct original research to find answers to their questions. This motivated students to use skills such as critical thinking, the scientific method, and collaboration to design solutions to problems.

Teacher as Co-Learner

Partner with and learn alongside students. Co-learning allows teachers to model the learning process by asking questions to which they genuinely want answers. It also shows students how adults research to develop a deep understanding of an issue or come up with a solution to a problem.

Marc Prensky (2010) talks about how educators can foster co-planning by engaging students in tasks normally completed solely by the teachers. He envisions students partnering with teachers to share the decision-making process for the curriculum. With the co-learning model, the values and expertise of all members of the class or community are harnessed. Teachers contribute the key concepts of the discipline and the learning-how-to-learn skills, and students bring their prior learning, world-view, and often, a propensity to learn about and use technology applications for learning.

For example, two teachers and three grade 4 students tried this model on a small scale with a pilot project called iPad Lunch. This group met weekly over lunch to discuss what was new with iPad apps. The students shared which apps they had purchased, and the teachers considered ways to use the suggested apps to enhance classroom learning. Through this co-learning model, the teachers valued and used the knowledge and expertise of all participants.

iPad Lunch had a dramatic effect on both teachers and students. For the teachers, it reinforced how important it is for students to be part of the decision-making process around what and how they learn. What really struck the teachers was how much the students liked being "let in on the secret" of how teachers plan the school day. Students were so excited when they saw their ideas were valued and represented in lesson plans.

This type of co-planning experience can also work in classrooms with older students. Under the guidance of teachers, students in university courses developed course syllabi, taught the classes, and self-assessed their learning. Students involved in this style of course described the actual experience as being even more important than the content. (Davidson 2014).

Teacher as Coach

Provide feedback to personalize learning. The teacher-as-coach model emphasizes delivering specific, descriptive feedback at regular intervals to students. For example, teachers can circulate to have conversations with individual students while they are working rather than marking work after it is completed. Keeping feedback timely ensures students do not practice mistakes. When teachers

During iPad Lunch, teachers and students discuss new apps.

focus their suggestions on one or two specific aspects of the work, students' revisions have a focus. We believe teachers can provide feedback in all areas of a child's life.

Paul Faggion, one of the grade 4 teachers in our school, is known for his coaching conversations with students about their social and emotional lives. When a student is dealing with a problem, he asks a series of questions to help the student arrive at possible solutions. Questioning sequences can sound like the following: So what happened at recess? Did Aaron tackle you during football? Are we allowed to tackle at school? What could you do next time if some of the boys start to tackle? What if they do not listen to you? What can you do? Are you comfortable to speak with Aaron about this incident now? What are you going to say to him? Do you need me to do anything to help?

2 / LEARNING HOW WE LEARN

What It Is

Many educators go into teaching with the vision of creating classrooms that develop critical, creative, and compassionate minds. The latest neuroscience on how the brain learns provides us with compelling research to help us do this. One of the most powerful insights coming out of brain research is that the brain is malleable — it can rewire and strengthen neural pathways in response to actions taken. We need to teach students to be aware of their cognitive faculties, how they work, and how to use them effectively. Teaching students about the importance of adopting a positive mindset toward learning and self-regulation can set them up for successful investigations.

Why It Is Important for Inquiry

Incorporating brain research and explicitly teaching mindfulness helps to promote a safe and inclusive atmosphere where students learn how to self-regulate their emotions and prepare to be inquirers. Exploring neuroscience with your students gives them the language to understand how their brains work and to act as advocates for the way they learn. Knowing the brain is malleable and that they can learn from their mistakes supports many aspects of inquiry learning. Students who are comfortable asking questions and teasing out the facets of an issue without the worry of making mistakes are willing to test their theories and reconsider previous hypotheses. Students who are not afraid to engage in real thinking are fluent in the process of learning, unlearning, and relearning new ideas.

PARTS OF THE BRAIN WE TEACH STUDENTS

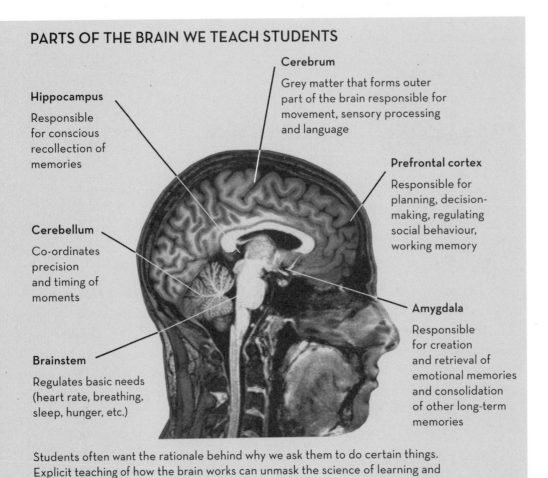

Hippocampus

Responsible for conscious recollection of memories

Cerebrum

Grey matter that forms outer part of the brain responsible for movement, sensory processing and language

Prefrontal cortex

Responsible for planning, decision-making, regulating social behaviour, working memory

Cerebellum

Co-ordinates precision and timing of moments

Amygdala

Responsible for creation and retrieval of emotional memories and consolidation of other long-term memories

Brainstem

Regulates basic needs (heart rate, breathing, sleep, hunger, etc.)

Students often want the rationale behind why we ask them to do certain things. Explicit teaching of how the brain works can unmask the science of learning and set the stage for inquiry.

Vision

So how does a classroom run on neuroscience look and sound? You might see students asking many questions, realizing that there are no "bad" ones. You might see students persisting through challenging activities and trying alternate ways to find an answer. Some teachers call their classrooms "mistakke zones" where mistakes are viewed as learning opportunities to be celebrated. Teachers might show how making mistakes supports inquiry and cultivates a mindset conducive to learning.

> MISTAKKE
> FREE
> ZONE

Challenge

The practice of making mistakes is not always valued in school. Often, failure is not seen as a first step in learning but as a barrier to trying new things.

TEACH NEUROPLASTICITY

Psychologist JoAnn Deak uses the analogy of elastic bands to explain the concept of neuroplasticity, i.e., how brains change over time. According to her metaphor, big elastic bands represent your strengths, or your aptitude, while smaller elastic bands are your skills that need to be worked and stretched to grow neural connections and pathways. Students often run into barriers working their smaller, underdeveloped pathways, resulting in discomfort. It can be easier to face challenging or difficult areas if you adopt a growth mindset. This mindset can often be motivating when students adopt the idea that they might not be able to perform a skill *yet*. In a grade 3 class, the learning-strategies teacher read Deak's book, *Your Fantastic Elastic Brain* (2010), and shared think-alouds about the workings of the brain. The students then identified the big elastic bands in their own lives (their strengths) and the smaller elastic bands (improvement areas) they wanted to develop through practice. Class discussion, goal setting, and the creation of a specific written plan helped each student improve.

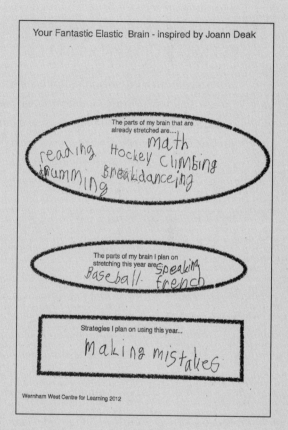

Your Fantastic Elastic Brain - inspired by Joann Deak

The parts of my brain that are already stretched are.....

reading Hockey Climbing math drumming breakdanceing

The parts of my brain I plan on stretching this year are speaking Baseball french

Strategies I plan on using this year...

making mistakes

Wernham West Centre for Learning 2012

What Steps Can You Take to Make Inquiry Happen for Your Students?

Our key strategy for fostering a supportive learning environment is to create a culture where students know themselves as learners. Taking time during lessons to reflect on mistakes and challenges helps students develop their metacognition and learn how to learn.

Cultivate a Growth Mindset

Research about a growth mindset builds on the neuroscience that our brain can change. Students who do not think their aptitude can change over time possess a fixed mindset. A student with a fixed mindset views intelligence as an immutable quality. Carol Dweck's years of research show students with a growth mindset are motivated to learn from their mistakes and see effort and practice as the key to the academic, social, and emotional gains they can make in their lives (2008).

Students with a growth mindset attribute their successes to the ability to adjust, practise, or ask an expert rather than rely on talent alone. Adopting a growth mindset can change one's outlook from "I'm no good at that," to "I can learn that if I use specific strategies." If students have an attitude that is open to learning, it can help them build on their natural strengths and ameliorate their weaknesses. It can help students persist with their work during challenging bouts and stick with tasks until they find creative solutions to problems.

Dear _____'s Brain,

Thank you for being my helpful Brain! I am going to keep organized by putting a calender on my board. Also I am going to exercise more by going for a run every day. Finaly I am going To sleep earlier so that I will wake up earlyer and have So much energy.

Thank you for helping me write This letter

Students wrote a letter to their brain explaining their sleep, exercise, and stress-reduction goals.

Practise adopting a growth mindset. Read books and show videos to tune students into the idea of a growth mindset so they realize we are all learners with our own individual set of strengths and weaknesses from which we can grow over time. For example, Janelle Monae's three-minute video on *Sesame Street*, the "Power of Yet," is a playful way for students to think about the power of a growth mindset. In the video, *Sesame Street* characters encounter problems performing a series of tasks. Monae, through song and dance, convinces them to identify their mistakes and make adjustments to achieve success. This video, or a similar one, can act as a springboard for discussion or role-play with students about how to unleash the "power of yet" in their own lives. Dance to the song with a group of kindergarteners, or have students write the lyrics to their own "power of yet" song. Help students make their own "yet" bracelets as a reminder to persist in times of challenge and doubt. Set goals with a growth mindset focus. Have students think about their areas of strength, how they can build on those, and how they can shore up areas of challenge.

"Yet" bracelets remind us that we have not mastered a skill, yet!

Teach Cognitive Control

Possessing the power to regulate your executive functioning skills, like paying attention, organizing, adjusting, and planning, is critical to learning. In times of high stress or emotion, it is difficult to regulate these skills and your brain can start to make decisions based on emotion instead of reason. When students learn about the functions of different parts of their brain, as well as strategies for self-regulation, they gain cognitive control. Students feel a sense of power and control over their learning. They can use this knowledge to regulate their emotions when necessary. Understanding how to calm the mind prepares students for exploring concepts in a clear and inquiry-ready way.

Keep the amygdala calm. Experiencing intense emotions and conflict is a natural part of school life. Collaborative work in the classroom engages different personalities with many opinions. When tensions rise, students need strategies to

Identifying the emotion you feel once your prefrontal cortex is disengaged is the first step to regaining cognitive control. To teach this, a grade 3 Health and Life Skills teacher, Martha Boyce, led students through a body scan exercise to help students identify where emotions live in their bodies. The students drew a body scan for visual representation. Some students coloured emotions on their hands while others coloured emotions in their heads. Doing a body scan to understand where emotions live in times of intensity is a good place to start for kids to be able to identify in their body where and why they are feeling upset or excited before they can reengage.

deal with their emotions so they can reengage in work. Brain research explains that when emotions run high and stress chemicals are released, they impair the prefrontal cortex, the higher-order thinking part of the brain responsible for planning and organizing. The stress chemicals cause the amygdala, the part of the brain involved in emotions, to regulate reactions (Siegel 2014). When this occurs, you might see a student walk away disgruntled from their group or take control of all the group's materials. Other students might start to argue with their partners and stop listening to ideas and or input. We need to find ways to calm the amygdala and reengage the prefrontal cortex so students can focus on their work. Deep breathing can help this process. With practice, we can manage the way our brain responds to emotional situations and return to learning in an efficient manner.

Value Mistakes

Help students understand that making mistakes can actually improve learning, because each time you fail you provide feedback to your brain. Failing at something gives students the opportunity to reflect on what went wrong, what went well, and what changes need to be implemented in similar situations. Learning from mistakes and from feedback also helps students to become adaptable and flexible. The term *failing well* promotes a mindset where students take responsibility for their actions, which can lead to self-reflection and independence over time (King 2009).

Identify mistakes that have led to positive results. Some strategies teachers can use to help students learn to take risks include:

› Learn about inventions borne out of mistakes.

› Have students identify crucial moments in their own lives when making a mistake led to new learning at school, through athletics, or through other activities.

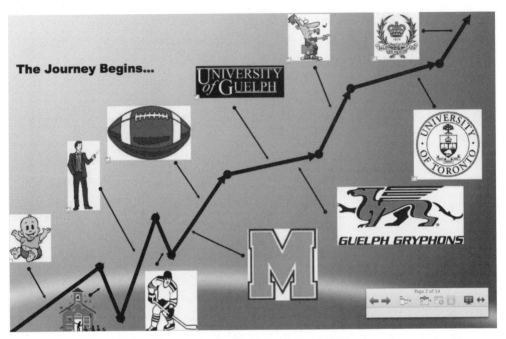

To build rapport with students and parents, Mr. Cav shares his Life Map, which illustrates where he has learned and grown from mistakes in his life.

› Model mistake making. We can show how making a mistake helped us to adopt a different direction in life. Grade 6 teacher JP Cavalluzzo shares stories from his life to introduce himself to parents on Curriculum Night. He provides information about mistakes he has made and how he overcame them as a way to model learning.

WHAT IT LOOKS LIKE IN THE CLASSROOM – KEEPING IN THE FLOW OF LEARNING

Grade 1 teacher Christie Gordon uses many techniques to keep students in the flow of learning. She started the year with an inquiry into the effect of choices students make at school every day. Through a variety of learning centres and investigations, the students explicitly practised specific social skills in collaborative groups. The teacher-librarian provided the class with books that

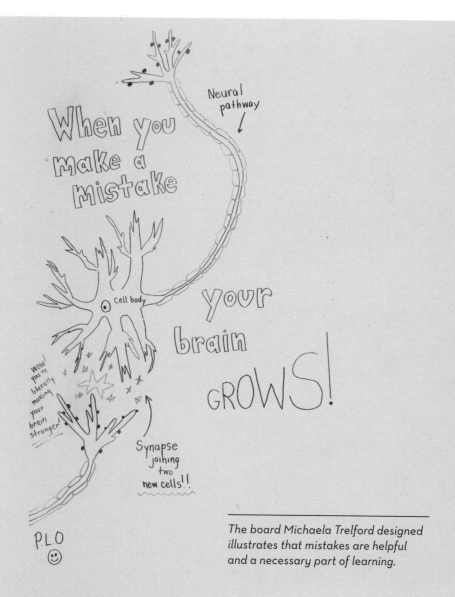

When you make a mistake your brain GROWS!

Neural pathway

Cell body

Wow! You're literally making your brain stronger.

Synapse joining two new cells!!

P.L.O ☺

The board Michaela Trelford designed illustrates that mistakes are helpful and a necessary part of learning.

included examples of cooperation and teamwork. Gordon introduced the picture book, *Have You Filled a Bucket Today?* by Carol McCloud and created a bucket centre for students to write optimistic and complimentary messages to fellow classmates throughout the day to show appreciation of their peers' strengths.

Fill someone's bucket with gratitude.

She herself practises mindfulness and has taught elements of this practice, including breathing exercises, to her students to help them to use it as a tool to stay calm. At prescribed times during the day, once they heard the cymbals or the class gong, students would stop and focus on their breathing. Books such as *Breathe* by Scott Magoon and *No Ordinary Apple* by Sara Marlowe helped to teach the concepts of helping others, practising gratitude, and exercising your empathy "muscles." The learning-strategies teacher provided specific input on how the brain learns and explained that practising deep breathing represents one way to train our brain to respond well to challenging situations.

Gordon also developed a Wellness Hour event. She invited guest speakers to take the students through different mindfulness activities that explored different aspects of empathy and cognitive control. The grade 1 students learned about the empathy centre in their brains (the right temporal parietal junction or RTPJ), the power of words to hurt, and how tone can alter the way our words are interpreted. A debrief with students about the Wellness Hour led to a brainstorm of action ideas. The students felt others would benefit from the knowledge they had gained. They created awareness posters to share their strategies with others at school and at home.

Students determined ways to strengthen different parts of their brain and shared their learning in the form of activity posters.

Assessment and Reflection Ideas

Encourage students to reflect on their thinking skills apart from the content they have learned. This gives students time to reflect on skills, like self-management, that can be used across many subjects.

> **I am BALANCED.** Sometimes I _get good_
> _marks_
> But other times I _make mistakes_

A grade 3 student reflects on how they are balanced.

OH SNAP! *Nothing is ever finished; always reflecting and revising*

Adopting a growth mindset, where you believe learning is a process and you can improve through practice and review, makes it easier to deal with your challenge areas. As teachers, we need to model making mistakes to reduce any stigma associated with failure. Why not organize a Mistake Spirit Week to create some energy and awareness to build the student body's comfort level for admitting and/or celebrating mistakes?

---

3 / TEACHER PREPARATION – CONCEPT-BASED TEACHING

What It Is

Many educators emphasize a concept-based approach to teaching and learning to address the crowded curriculum and introduce students to real-world issues. Concepts are big ideas, and many specific examples exist for every concept in a range of disciplines; they are universal and timeless. We can find many specific examples in math, language, the arts, music, science, social sciences, and so on. Because concepts are transferable and enduring, they help students grasp a bigger picture of the world.

Selecting appropriate concepts to focus on is important, because it drives the direction of the unit. For example, a unit about ecosystems that focuses on change vs. interrelationships will go in different directions.

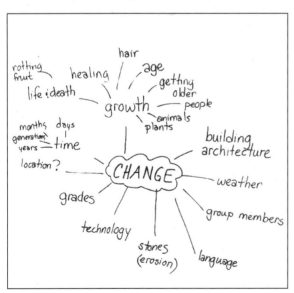

This web illustrates a number of topics in different subject areas that connect to the concept of change.

CONCEPTS - ABSTRACT, TIMELESS, UNIVERSAL	SPECIFIC EXAMPLES THAT CAN BE USED TO ILLUSTRATE A CONCEPT
measurement	slope, line, velocity
celebrations	Quebec Winter Carnival
conflict	War of 1812
systems	conservation of energy, digestion
power	the fur trade
responsibility	UN Sustainable Development Goals
perspective	first contact, exploration, discoveries
change	life cycles, states of matter
extinction	dinosaurs
metaphor	poetry
conservation	water cycle
democracy	federal government
technology	ancient Rome
causation	simple machines
patterns	genetics
interrelationships	ecosystems
sustainability	electricity generation
adaptations	camouflage
character	biographies
choice	gang mentality
mental health	teen depression
innovation	green industry
ergonomics	movement

Many curriculum documents are starting to include concepts. Teachers can determine specific concepts appropriate to their subject area related to the knowledge and skills in their curriculum.

Outside of school, the world does not exist in strict disciplines. Even with rigorous curriculum documents, there remains a lot of scope for teachers to select the concepts they feel are most appropriate for the age and stage of their students. Concepts can be examined from multiple perspectives and in different subject areas within your own

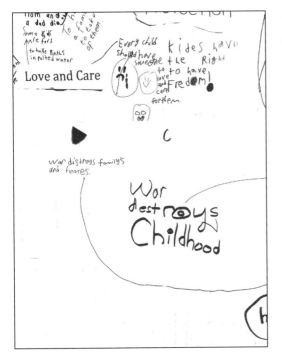

Love and Care

classroom. When determining learning goals, consider what it is you really want students to know, understand, and be able to do by the end of a unit. Look at all the required skills and knowledge to ascertain *why* they are important for students to learn. Rather than focusing solely on learning facts and skills, strive for deep, conceptual understanding that can be transferred across disciplines.

In any given unit, we have found the ideal number of concepts seems to be between two and four. When more concepts are selected, units become too wide-ranging, and remaining focused becomes a challenge. When too few are selected, the unit tends to lack real-world connections.

Once the concepts are determined, teachers can then figure out how best to teach and connect skills and knowledge in the curriculum.

Why It Is Important for Inquiry

Choosing to focus units and lessons on concepts rather than on facts and skills keeps the learning goals more explicit. Rather than learning skills and facts in isolation, concept-based teaching and learning allows teachers and students to manage the many curriculum expectations and tackle world issues. Facts and skills are used to access content and deepen understanding. In a concept-based classroom, students explore specific examples that exist in the curriculum and connect to the real world. Such context increases student engagement and is more likely to lead to long-term mastery. The following chart shows how real-world issues, facts, and skills can be used in concert to help students unpack conceptual understanding.

REAL-WORLD ISSUE		
Concept	Concept	Concept
Facts and Skills	Facts and Skills	Facts and Skills

From my curriculum documents

Concept-based teaching keeps learning focussed on transferable understandings that can be applied in different contexts and disciplines —they can be applied to other subject areas without the need to reteach it, reinforcing concepts for students and saving teachers time. For example, grade 9 drama teacher Judith McDonnell knew that she wanted her students to explore a multitude of concepts through an issues-based curriculum. She shared the true story of a brutal, racially motivated gang attack on a Bengali student. Her students uncovered the concepts of perspective, nativism, and courage while building their knowledge of drama forms as well as creation, presentation, and reflection skills. Building empathy underpinned all of the work developed. They tried on the roles of different characters in the news story to understand how context and other factors drove this hate crime. The students' heightened understanding of these concepts in the arts can be applied in other subject areas when exploring any issue.

Engaging problem we can use to plan action

Abstract idea that is transferable

REAL-WORLD ISSUE – RACIALLY MOTIVATED GANG ATTACK					
perspective		nativism		courage	
Drama – use role play to explore, develop, and represent themes, ideas, characters, feelings, and beliefs in producing drama works	Civics – describe some civic issues of local, national, and/or global significance	Drama – identify and explain the various purposes that drama serves or has served in diverse communities and cultures from the present and past	Civics – compare the perspectives of different groups on selected issues	Drama – identify specific social skills and personal characteristics they have acquired or stengthened through drama work that can help them succeed in other areas of life	Civics – explain how various actions can contribute to the common good at the local, national, and/or global level

From my curriculum documents

Vision

What does the process look like? In a concept-based classroom you might see teachers reviewing curriculum documents together to determine which concepts would be appropriate for the age and stage of their students. Teachers meet to plan who will introduce students to various concepts and how they will teach concepts in an interdisciplinary way. Students explore concepts critically and come up with creative and sometimes out-of-the-box approaches to issues.

Challenge

Sometimes your curriculum can feel like you are running through a laundry list of knowledge and skills instead of teaching through concepts. We often want to have through lines of ideas so our teaching centres on enduring understandings, and we can connect with the other teachers who work with our students.

What Steps Can You Take to Make Inquiry Happen for Your Students?

Teachers can start down the road to inquiry-based teaching by beginning to blur the lines between disciplines. Teachers can call their community together to make plans for their students. A planning partner provides support and allows for brainstorming more concepts to explore. By meeting with colleagues, teachers can work together to plan how students can develop a deep understanding of concepts across disciplines. Collaborating with colleagues to manage workload during the inquiry process means more can be accomplished in less time. For example, a drama teacher worked with the librarian to help students conduct research on Bethnal Green in the 1990s and the social and economic unrest resulting from high unemployment rates and an influx of new immigrants. This learning in the library informed their role plays in drama class.

Start with the End in Mind

If you don't know where you are heading, how will you know when you get there or if you are making progress toward your goal? Although teachers using an inquiry-based model are responsive to student questions that may change the direction of the units, it is still important to start with a plan. In an inquiry-based classroom, plans remain flexible, student input is gathered along the way, and you may explore things you hadn't considered at the outset – but direction and goals are still required. Year-long plans that link the content in different disciplines are vital. Before embarking on teaching a unit, teachers need to consider what concepts they want students to understand and what skills they would like them to have mastered by the end. After these are determined, teachers can then craft a plan for getting there. This process of backward design always begins with the end in mind (Wiggins and McTighe 1999).

Prioritize Your Learning Goals

Curriculum documents usually provide an extensive list of what students should know and be able to do by the end of the school year. Teachers need to determine the best order to introduce new concepts and how much time to spend learning new skills and deepening understanding. For example, teachers meet at the start or end of the school year to make links between their curricula and plan both how and when specific concepts can be addressed in the various subject areas. Shorter meetings to check in about the plan can be scheduled throughout the year to make any adjustments.

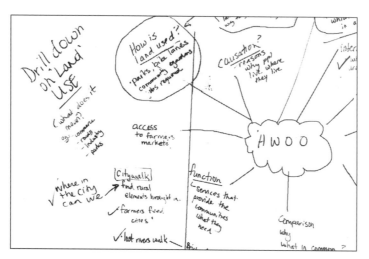

Collaboratively, teachers determine how to sequence the teaching of various concepts and issues connected to employment and land use.

Develop Learning Engagements that Achieve Multiple Purposes

In the classroom, teachers are in control of the time spent on any one part of the curriculum. Since time is always at a premium, teach several expectations simultaneously rather than teaching skills and content in isolation. This allows students to make connections between different disciplines, develop skills in multiple subject areas, and saves teachers time. Science and social studies can often provide a context for language or numeracy work. By determining which expectations can logically be grouped and taught together, we can create multidisciplinary conceptual units. For example, grade 7 students were tasked with debating an idiom. One group had to convince others that "over the long term, the carrot is better than the stick." They needed to support their argument with evidence gathered from the novel they were reading in English class, specific examples from their Canadian history class, and connections between historical events and the present day. According to Alicia, a student who worked on this project, they needed to use their research skills, learn the importance of going back and reviewing class notes, practise presentation skills, use collaboration skills to work with a partner, and learn how formal debates worked – all expectations from the curriculum.

Map Your Curriculum

If you are going to chunk your curriculum into sections where logically connected expectations are taught together, you will need to find a way to track what and when everything is taught. Commercial curriculum mapping tools or your own spreadsheets can help all teachers track what they have covered from year to year and help ensure that each strand is covered.

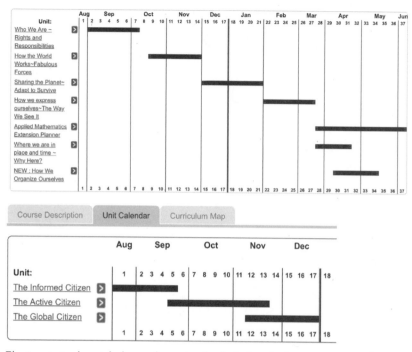

Unit:	Aug	Sep	Oct	Nov	Dec	Jan	Feb	Mar	Apr	May	Jun

Course Description | **Unit Calendar** | Curriculum Map

	Aug	Sep	Oct	Nov	Dec	
Unit:	1	2 3 4 5 6	7 8 9 10	11 12 13 14	15 16 17	18
The Informed Citizen ▶						
The Active Citizen ▶						
The Global Citizen ▶						
	1	2 3 4 5 6	7 8 9 10	11 12 13 14	15 16 17	18

Electronic tools can help you keep track of what and when you are teaching particular units.

OH SNAP! *Nothing is ever finished; always reflecting and revising*

Even when you are just starting to teach through inquiry, collaboration is highly recommended. Planning together with colleagues leads to more ideas for both teaching and assessing concepts. Work together with other educators who also teach your students to craft a common approach to concepts in diverse subject areas. If you are teaching through inquiry on your own, it helps to have a planning partner to share ideas.

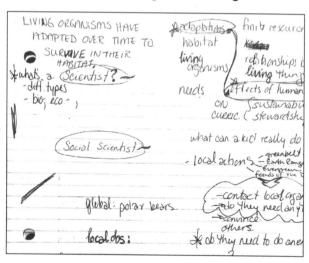

Notes teachers made while planning together include multiple subject areas and approaches.

4 / HOW CAN WE OBSERVE AND GET TO KNOW AN ISSUE? THE ROLE OF PROVOCATIONS

What It Is

A provocation is an activity that piques a student's curiosity and drives genuine questions. Activities designed to foster curiosity help students formulate questions and activate prior knowledge about a concept or issue. Through provocations, teachers can help students connect to and deepen thinking about an issue. To quickly get to a point where genuine, compelling questions are being asked, start with an engaging provocation.

Effective provocations help students care about the concept being studied by eliciting wonder and spurring a desire for more information. We encourage teachers to engage as many senses as possible in provocations and create experiential learning engagements that capture students' imaginations and challenge their perceptions. Provocations can play a powerful role in sparking and developing compassionate

The students watched eggs under lights in an incubator warm up and eventually hatch. Students cared for the baby chicks in the classroom.

thinking. By experiencing a concept, students can feel the emotion, awe, and wonder connected to the concept they are studying.

Why It Is Important for Inquiry

Children are naturally inquisitive. Teachers can leverage this curiosity by finding engaging ways to activate students' thinking about concepts. Effective provocations can activate the prior knowledge students have about a concept and help them to start to think about questions they initially want to explore. Teachers who use inquiry need to thoughtfully consider how to spark interest in units and how to challenge students to wonder throughout a unit. Sharing provocations during a unit helps to deepen thinking and uncover and use student questions in the unit.

Dr. Math dressed up in scrubs to get students excited about learning the concept of the "order of operations."

During provocations, teachers can observe and document students' thoughts and skill development by taking photos or video or by making anecdotal notes. They can do this on their own, as they monitor individuals or small groups, or they can invite other teachers to assist with the documentation, to ensure all key student reactions are captured. Having this documentation is useful not only for students to refer back to, but also for the teacher to use to confirm student understanding, interests, and questions and to plan the next learning engagements.

Vision

What does this process look like? To provide interesting provocations before units on light or time, students might arrive at school one day to find the whole classroom darkened for the first hour or lacking any working clocks. Teachers document the comments students make about the absence of light or awareness of time and lead a class discussion to debrief the experience. Teachers ask if there were any issues that could arise out of not knowing the time, and students build on one another's ideas and comments. The teacher reflects on the conversation to judge what students already know about the topic and create further interest about the concepts of time, sequences, or patterns.

Challenge

Sometimes we do not plan provocations, because they seem like a huge effort with little gain. It can be onerous to get parental permission forms signed and to plan activities outside of the building.

You don't have to go far. Use your school grounds to investigate local flora and fauna. Spending time outdoors can foster an appreciation of natural beauty.

What Steps Can You Take to Make Inquiry Happen for Your Students?

Teachers need to be keen observers during provocations. We need to listen for and gather data about student wonderings, current levels of understanding, and misconceptions. We need to use this data to generate questions, such as the following, to determine what to do next:

› What do students understand about the concept or issue? Do they have enough background knowledge to move forward, or is more background needed? How can we build on what they know?

› What questions are students really asking? For young students, this may sometimes need to be deciphered from the types of comments they are making. Prompts like "Tell me more about that" can help get the clarification teachers require to move forward. During kindergarten inquiry time, for example, the teacher heard the following comment, "I'm going to measure Scooby-Doo," and turned this into the question, "How big is Scooby-Doo?" Another student stated "I'm going to try the magnet – that one doesn't stick." The teacher interpreted this statement as the student inquiring about what magnets can and cannot pick up.

› Do student queries link to other parts of the curriculum? With what other teachers should we collaborate to help students discover the answers to their questions? Should we share specific questions with teachers of other subjects so they can explore them with students in their classes?

Engage Students' Emotions to Inspire Awe and Wonder

We want students to care about the concepts and issues they explore because, if they truly wonder about something, then they are in a better frame of mind to learn about it, ask genuine questions, and invest the time needed to find answers to their questions. The goal is for students to feel immersed in learning: to involve their senses, appreciate the beauty of the world, and be moved to take action.

Lead with concepts. Most curriculum documents are filled with specific expectations that describe the skills and knowledge students should learn at any given grade. For students embarking on a unit of study about rights and responsibilities, for.example, teachers kicked off a study of the universal right to water through by exploring the concept of conservation. As a provocation, students were asked to bring in samples or images of water that were important to them. Students brought in samples of lake water, water from religious sources, as well as images of family vacations and special habitats. This allowed students to identify with

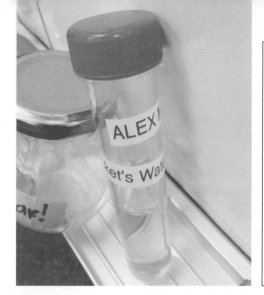

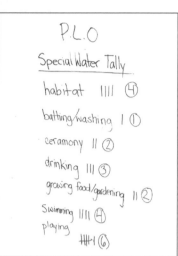

P.L.O

Special Water Tally

habitat   llll   ④

bathing/washing   l   ①

ceramony   ll   ②

drinking   lll   ③

growing food/gardening   ll   ②

Swimming   llll   ④

playing   ⑪ l   ⑥

Students brought in many examples of special water from different places and experiences in their lives and tallied the sources of water they valued.

the preciousness of water before exploring how easy or challenging it can be to access it in different places, and to reflect on the need for conservation.

Use provocations throughout a unit. Sometimes teachers plan provocations only at the launch of a unit. Since provocations can be so powerful, teachers can challenge students further when they develop provocations *throughout* a unit. For example, in the midst of a unit focused on the concept of consequences, provocations set a scene for students starting a novel study. Books from the Akimbo series by Alexander McCall Smith are set in Africa and describe the adventures Akimbo and his father experience living and working on a game reserve. Grade 3 teachers created a scene

in the hallway using artifacts that reflected key details from the text. The scene included pictures of animals that live on game reserves and Masai warriors from the region, as well as maps of the African continent. Students observed the scene and recorded questions and observations. They asked questions about the artifacts. In the debrief, some students did not understand the concept of poaching and its impact on certain animal populations, so that was explored further. Teachers can plan new provocations to clear up misunderstandings or to provide more background information through guest speakers, newspaper articles, or related texts to make the concept of poaching clear.

Clear up misconceptions. When teachers are aware of all the expectations in their curriculum documents, they have more flexibility when planning provocations. Knowing what is in the curriculum allows teachers to respond to student needs and interests and determine when new skills should be practised. For example, teachers made a plan to visit an outdoor education centre for a water walk – they wanted their grade 3 students to experience what it was like for children with no indoor plumbing or easy access to water to get the daily amount of water their family required. In response to this, teachers created a new provocation linked to a math expectation about using tallies that challenged students to count and record all the places they could access fresh water in the school. Knowing the math expectations needed to be met helped determine the way in which the new provocation was designed to help build empathy before the planned trip to take the water walk. Change is possible when teachers know their curriculum and are willing to be flexible.

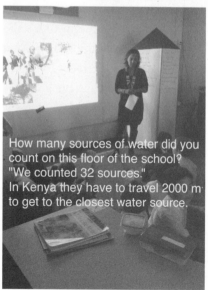

How many sources of water did you count on this floor of the school? "We counted 32 sources."
In Kenya they have to travel 2000 m to get to the closest water source.

We planned this additional provocation about the water walk because we wanted to ensure students understood their own easy access to potable water.

A student remarked, "This water walk made me feel angry. I can't believe that kids my age have to walk this distance many times a day to get water for their family instead of going to school."

Spark empathy. When students empathize, they are more likely to be motivated to help improve the lives of others. If teachers can create situations where students put themselves in other people's shoes, students are more willing to investigate reasons and possible solutions to solve injustices. To want to help others, students need to be able to consider how others feel about different situations and circumstances. For example, when the grade 3 students visited the outdoor education centre to simulate the water walk mentioned above, walking two kilometres along an uneven, rocky path with heavy buckets opened their eyes to what life can be like for children without easy access to water. Through debrief discussions with teachers, the students understood how daily walks to source water affect children living in developing countries.

Leverage student interests. Teachers can use student passions as a springboard for learning. For example, before a history unit focusing on continuity and change, students could compare how their favourite sports were played in the past with how they are played today. Teachers pose questions such as, "What if anything about the game has changed? What has stayed the same? Are the athletes in baseball, for example, wearing the same equipment? Have the rules of the game changed? Are there co-ed leagues now that did not exist before?" Investigating a topic familiar to the students can lead to understanding concepts and modelling historical thinking.

Engage students in real-world issues. Discussing current events allows students to develop opinions, challenge perceptions, and learn more about the world. A news article or broadcast can be used as a provocation to provide background information about a subject, inspire awe, stimulate compassion, or gauge a student's background knowledge.

For example, a report about a work of art stolen during the Second World War, and whether or not it should be returned to Austria, spurred questions related to a number of concepts. Students wondered, "What do you do if the artwork from a personal collection ends up in a museum? What is the process for aggrieved parties to make a claim of ownership? Who can help support the retrieval of missing artwork, and what process can you follow to get it back?" Their discussion and responses to the report informed the planning and flow of subsequent lessons. The widespread availability of news on the Internet makes it easier to access and discuss real-world issues from multiple perspectives.

Work with Primary Sources

Exploring a concrete object sometimes provides a portal to another place or time. When students use their senses to examine tangible objects, the exploration process and observations can spark questions about abstract concepts.

Use images and infer. Showing images relating to the unit and discussing them can help orient students to a topic, as well as build a common vocabulary for the class. Images engage learners of all ages and stages. Students often want to read or write to learn more about the topic (despite the complexity of these tasks). For example, in a grade 2 classroom before a unit about local history, the teacher showed an archival image of the local community. Students gathered clues about the image and tried to determine where and when it was taken. They learned how analyzing images can give you a sense of time and place. Through such a provocation, students describe what they see, hypothesize about what is happening, and pose questions about information

Blog Buddies

Form 2 is Thinking Critically!

Posted on December 10, 2014

To kick start our newest unit of inquiry, Then and Now, the boys were given this picture to discuss and 'think critically' about. In small groups, the boys became detectives as they asked each other questions about 'when' and 'where' this picture scene may have taken place. They came up with wonderful ideas and challenged each other to prove whether this was a picture from the past, present or future and why. They provided evidence about

Recent P

- Taking a Wal
  Lane
- 2F LOVES In
  Really?
- What Makes
- Blogging the
  Change!
- Guided Read
  Literacy

Recent (

- Click on Wha
  Giggle?
- Mujib Adam a
  You Giggle?
- Year 2.1 on **P
  Password P**
- Lawrence Da
  Making Pum
- Paulish on **H
  Helps Us To**

These types of resources can be found at a local library, municipal archive, or online.

Artifacts like this *shofar* can encourage children to talk about ideas ranging from religions to family customs and traditions.

they want to learn. The students did not observe any jails in the picture and wondered whether or not they existed at this time. They were also intrigued about whose responsibility it was to maintain law and order in the 1900s.

Analyze artifacts. Artifacts and objects can also spur inquiry. For example, in a unit about traditions, students and teachers brought in artifacts that represented something that was important to their family. Many of the artifacts students brought in ended up being religious or cultural. For example, one student brought in a *shofar* (a ram's horn used in Jewish New Year observances) to share with his classmates. The other students explored the physical characteristics of the artifact and asked questions about it to determine its purpose. The owner then described how it was used at home and why it was important to his family. This provocation allowed for a deeper discussion about how perspectives of class members may differ. Although it was not a part of the planned teaching, some students became interested in learning more about different religions. The teacher and librarian made several texts available for students to advance their thinking. From there, students could check their hypotheses, or wonder some more. An artifact like the *shofar* can spark inquiry that leads to questions surrounding many concepts, such as traditions, spirituality, and family. Students may want to work independently to explore some of these concepts further and follow up with their own research. For more information on managing student questions, see chapter 5.

Assessment and Reflection Ideas

Before teaching new skills and concepts, consider how best to assess current levels of student understanding. By taking the time to diagnose levels of conceptual understanding and skill mastery, teachers can save time, as they do not have to reteach students what they already know. If, for example, students already know the states of matter or how to write an explanation, then teachers can skip that part of their plan and move on to the next planned exploration of concepts and skills. Diagnostic assessment may occur at the beginning of a unit, but it can also happen whenever a new skill or concept is introduced.

Students often forget they didn't always know something. Documenting thinking at the beginning, in the middle, and at the end of a unit helps them to more accurately reflect on their learning. If student thoughts from the beginning of the unit are made visible, then students can refer back to previously learned concepts. Elementary teacher Mark Ferley installed more whiteboards in his classroom so the day's thinking and learning could be documented without having to erase anything. He then spends time at the end of the day referring back to key concepts and ideas that were covered.

Other teachers use anchor charts to explain key concepts, word walls for vocabulary building, and portfolios to document student thinking over time. There are lots of ways to do this.

```
Ways we can start a
paragraph to summarize a chapter
of a book.

1. This book is about...

2. In this book...
         story....

3. Charlotte's Web is...
```

```
Ways we can start
sentences in the body of
a paragraph.

1. First...
2. Next...
3. After/Then...
4. Lastly/Finally...
```

Teachers often choose to reference some of the key concepts captured on the whiteboards at the end of the day to help students remember and consolidate their thinking.

```
Good Readers INFER

You infer when you
use your prior knowledge
and clues from the text
to figure out what the author
means ("read between the lines")

* I think the author means...
* It doesn't say so on the
    page but it means...
* The author said___. That
    means...
```

```
What Makes A Good Report?

Descriptive words
Scientific words — explained
Informational — to learn/teach
Avoid opinion
Catchy introduction   — fact
                       — quote
                       ` question
Organized paragraphs — what it is
                      — how it works
                      — how it is changing
Satisfying ending
```

Anchor charts can be developed with students and then posted for reference as a way to reinforce criteria.

OH SNAP! *Nothing is ever finished; always reflecting and revising*

Simple provocations can make a big impact. Scavenger hunts and other short walks with your class can serve as an easy provocation. Some teachers ask parents to sign a blanket "neighbourhood tour" permission slip so that they can take their students on short, frequent excursions. Students might go into the field to estimate its perimeter and area or to measure the heights of different flowers in the garden of a neighbourhood park. Walks around the school or neighbourhood, looking for examples of shapes in the environment, led grade 1 students to notice common shapes in architectural features and wonder why many roofs have a triangular shape.

5 / HOW CAN WE TEASE OUT THE FACETS OF THE PROBLEM OR ISSUE? BUILDING THINKING SKILLS

What It Is

The process of teasing out the facets represents a crucial part of inquiry. Building thinking skills such as asking questions, trying to find answers, and realizing you are missing information or skills to fully understand an issue is key at this point. Exploring new avenues, asking more questions to gain a fuller understanding, doing more research, and comparing personal findings to peers or experts help students determine their own conclusions based on evidence.

Thinking is required to formulate questions and to answer them effectively.

Teachers ask questions, together with students, to deepen critical, creative, and compassionate thinking. Questions are key to research. They drive the investigative process and lead to understanding the crux of an issue. Good questions often can't be answered with a yes or no, as they require research to answer. Good questions help us uncover different points of view about an issue.

QUESTIONS THAT REPRESENT THE 3Cs OF THINKING		
Critical Thinking › requires research to answer › considers multiple perspectives	**Creative Thinking** › requires outside-the-box ideas to answer › considers new options	**Compassionate Thinking** › requires empathy to answer › considers making a difference in individual, local, or global communities
Is nuclear energy a clean energy source? Can biomass be bad for the environment, and if, yes, how? How good is nuclear energy for the environment? Is it 100% eco-friendly? How can we make biomass more environmentally friendly? What is the best source of energy to use to power our cars?	What new ideas for energy are there? How can we make a hydrogen bomb safer? How can we make nuclear energy better? How can we make nuclear energy safer and more effective?	How does the burning of coal and oil affect the environment? How can everyone on Earth be safe? How can we stop killing birds with windmills? How can we make an impact? How can we make geothermal energy safe from earthquakes?

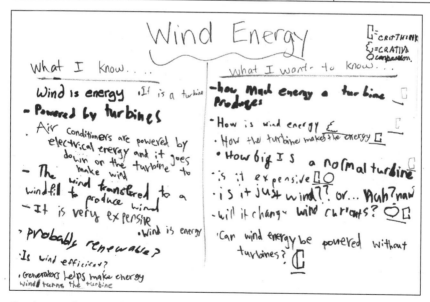

Grade 5 students explored how we harness energy to make electricity and categorized their questions according to the three Cs of thinking.

Why It Is Important for Inquiry

The process of learning, unlearning, and relearning drives inquiry. If students are asking questions, they can look at issues from multiple points of view before developing their own. Starting with student questions ensures we build on their current levels of understanding. Sometimes questions can be answered through books or online research, but at other times a survey, experiment, or interview might be more effective. Delving into researchable questions helps students and teachers test current thinking and dispel myths. Thinking about findings and asking further questions leads to a deeper understanding of an issue.

Vision

What could this process look like? Students ask a variety of questions, conduct research to better understand an issue, and share their findings. They interrogate their evidence asking, "Does this seem right? What am I learning from this piece of evidence?"

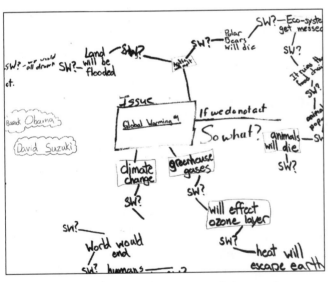

Students worked in small groups to ask the question "So what?" multiple times to get at the effects of global warming.

Students share their research findings with one another, discuss the root causes of an issue, and support their opinions with facts they have learned. Questions that arise from conversations with teachers and peers are targeted for further research. You might hear questions like, "So what?" or "What is significant about this piece of information or evidence?" and prompts like, "Tell me more" or "Why do you think so?" modelled and practised.

Challenge

We start out Monday morning with our teacher questions about a concept. Within a short while, the discussion falls flat. Students do not always have enough background information to ask insightful, concept-based questions. This can leave teachers feeling like they are directing the conversation, rather than having the students share their information and ideas.

CHARACTER COACHING THROUGH QUESTIONS

› Keep conversations in the zone of proximal development; start with what students know, then push beyond to add new information. For example, digital citizenship is part of the technology curriculum, and some students in middle school were struggling with online group work. The vice principal's questioning sequence with the students went like this: "What was your task to do online? If you are working collaboratively, how should you communicate with each other? Should we call each other names even as a joke? Why not? What agreements can we develop so that we can ensure that we all work together effectively online?"

› Provide an environment in which students are not dissuaded by failure. If their initial questions do not yield rich results, coach them to start again with a new question. A basketball player asked the coach, "Do you think we are going to win?" Instead, the coach encouraged them to ask, "What strategies can we use as a team to create scoring opportunities?"

What Steps Can You Take to Make Inquiry Happen for Your Students?

Teachers are great at asking questions; the challenge is to stop asking so many questions ourselves and to create opportunities for students to ask them. In Bold School classrooms, students provide the bulk of the discussion so their voices, ideas, and hypotheses are respected. The role of the teacher is to facilitate these discussions and challenge thinking. When students struggle with understanding a concept, the teacher can step in to provide the missing information or guide students toward understanding. Shifting who asks the questions from teacher to student can promote a range of ideas to explore. Ideally, we want teachers and students working together to ask questions that promote deeper thinking on an issue.

Encourage Students to Ask Questions

Classroom discussions provide a forum for students to share their hypotheses, gain feedback from others, and clarify their own thinking. Students need coaching on what constitutes an effective question so they can retrieve the information they need. This is not a skill that can be taught and learned in one course or one semester, as questions are a way of approaching teaching and learning at all grade levels. It is through repeated exposure to questioning that we believe students learn to be inquirers.

For example, high-school teacher Fiona Marshall taught her students to ask researchable questions. In Civics, students began to research an issue and then drafted 10 to 12 questions. She provided feedback on the questions to ensure they adhered to the criteria, which included being narrow enough to have a specific answer (not "it depends") and contained definable terms. She then modelled three possible questions as an exemplar, and students refined their original questions (they could not use hers). As students conducted their research, they modified their questions as they learned new information.

Resist the Urge to Overplan

Pre-planning activities sometimes takes away from the time needed to investigate student questions. Some teachers find it best to plan the provocations to get at the key concepts and then explore questions that come up in response to these prompts. For example, grade 10 students worked in small groups and shared what they knew about a topic using a chart titled "What I Think I Know." In their group, they then discussed each point using background information and experiences. When the group agreed that a statement was true, they moved it to a new chart titled "What I Now Know." When there was no consensus, they posted it on the "What I Don't

Know" chart. This valued each student's thinking and allowed students to build on one another's ideas.

Take notes on **AT LEAST 4 OF THE ARTICLES**

◊ Make sure your notes are clear, in your own words, specific AND organized under different categories like the ones below:

    a) **The positive aspects of the oil sands**
    b) **The negative effects of the oil sands**
    c) **Various proposals for managing the oil sands**

      Print out a copy of these notes for Harkness day so that you can refer to these. These notes will be handed in to your teacher for assessment.

      Write **TWO QUESTIONS** which you can ask your peers with an eye to furthering the discussion and increasing the class' understanding of the issue. These questions must be different than mine.

Some teachers post questions electronically to encourage critical thinking.

Coach Students on How to Ask an Effective Question

Being able to ask effective questions and think about a particular topic or issue are key skills in today's digital world. Fiona Marshall worked with students in grade 11 to co-create curriculum. With practice and feedback, students got better at asking questions and learned to lead with their questions. Each student was responsible for conducting a 45-minute seminar on a particular issue. In preparing the seminar, students were required to assign readings and develop questions to lead the group discussions. For assessment, the students needed to prepare quizzes for their peers. At this stage of schooling, the hope is that students have developed thinking skills to ask the difficult questions required to unpack concepts in particular disciplines.

Manage Questions Throughout a Unit

The issue of how to best manage student questions also arises. Teachers need to create structures that allow students to pose and explore their own questions, as well as address questions required by the teacher. If students generate a number of questions they want to explore, teachers need a system to pursue a number of questions simultaneously. For example, grade 3 teachers Mark Ferley and David Osorio created templates to help each student develop open-ended questions, conduct research, and confer with their teachers on their findings. After an investigation was complete, students extended their learning by taking action or asking and investigating another question.

Unit of Inquiry

Question

Teacher approved for open-ended criteria

| N | Y |

Personal hypothesis based on present understanding. Explain what you believe the answer might be based on what you already know.

CHOOSE YOUR OWN INQUIRY PATH....

Based on what I now know, I am going to choose to:

Take Action / Create Further Questions

This system helps students to investigate their questions within their zone of proximal development.

Posting questions for everyone to see provides a space for revision and reflection.

Post student questions. Create opportunities to pose and record questions that arise throughout the unit. Posting student questions keeps thinking visible for reference by all members of the class. Some teachers maintain an inquiry board in the classroom or online discussion forums. As the unit progresses, and the students' learning deepens, you can go back to tweak, explore, or discard earlier questions. It is often only after students know something about the topic that they can ask deeper, more complex questions.

Prioritize and group questions. Combine similar questions together rather than juggling multiple questions. Choose five or six of the meatiest questions that target identified concepts to investigate and to focus the discussion.

Where do rocks come from?

Where did this come from?

Did this come from the sea?

Are some rocks found underground?

Do all rocks come from mines?

Where do you find minerals and crystals?

Why does this look like it came from a volcano?

Where can I find this rock?

Where do rocks come from?

Are some minerals from space?

Do all rocks come from the same place?
. . .

How do scientists find the rocks?

What is water made of? Ryder, JP, Peter
What is the water cycle and why is it useful?

Why are oceans and lakes important? How do waves form? Xander, Xavier, Fateh, Wilson

Why is water important to living things? Adrian, Jeremy, Fredrik (humans & animals) / Arthur, Malcolm, Gordon

How is water filtered so we can drink it? Malek, Metcalfe, DeLuca, Kyle

Where does water come from? Alex, Matty, Ryan

Assigning your students to research groups helps to share the workload.

ACCEPT STUDENT QUESTIONS THROUGHOUT A LESSON

With every interaction, verbal and nonverbal, teachers send subtle and not-so-subtle messages to students about what is valued. Waiting until the end of a lesson to respond to student questions can send the message that information the teacher holds is more important than the student's question. Students should feel like partners in the learning, so teachers need to be aware of any hidden messages they send.

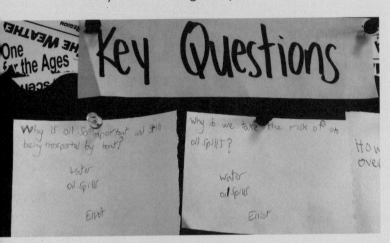

After collaborative discussion, more complex questions emerge.

WHAT IT LOOKS LIKE IN THE CLASSROOM—EXPERIMENTATION

Students in grade 4 conducted several experiments to classify what constitutes a physical change and what constitutes a chemical change. They stretched elastic bands and classified that action as a physical change. They melted sugar, which broke the chemical bonds, to learn about a chemical change. Working with peers during lab time, they built on one another's ideas and did not wait for approval from the teacher before proceeding through every step of the experiment. The teacher circulated between groups to help where needed and made note of questions the students asked as they worked. At the end of the period, the teacher posted the questions she had overheard. The students then had a discussion about their wonderings regarding physical and chemical changes in the world. As a group, they determined which of their questions would be researchable and how each question might be answered. In subsequent classes, the teacher helped groups of students answer their questions using different methods. Finally, the teacher acted as a facilitator and challenged students to determine if the process of mummification represented a physical or chemical change. This sparked a debate among students, who researched print and Internet resources to confirm their thinking after their own series of experiments.

Develop a Research Practice

The ability to know how to investigate a number of sources and evaluate their worthiness is an important life skill. From an early age, students should analyze a range of both primary and secondary sources to develop their thinking skills.

Use a variety of resources. Share resources with students that look at issues from multiple perspectives, and teach students to carefully consider the resources they use. For example, when researching maps, a variety of projections help students understand there are different ways of presenting visual information. Creation stories from different cultures also allow students to compare common or different ideas. Students benefit when teachers present many views of the world.

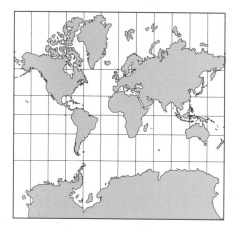

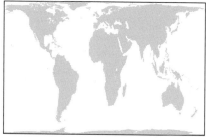

Viewing multiple types of maps allows students to see how the globe can be represented in different ways. The Gall-Peters projection map (above) more accurately represents each continent's relative size, and the Mercator projection (left) more accurately represents the angles between landmasses.

EVALUATING RESOURCES

Information is everywhere, and students need to learn whether or not the sources they are exploring are reputable. Here are some tips for determining the validity of sources:

› Who is the author? Are they experts in the subject matter? The information is more likely to be credible if it is the author's job to research or teach this information than if it is a personal blog or opinion.

› Is it a trusted organization, such as an encyclopedia or news source, that adheres to research and/or journalistic standards? For online sources, check the URL carefully. If the address includes a tilde (~), then it indicates it is likely a personal page within a larger organization.

› Is the information factual, or is it the author's opinion? Can other sources of information support what you are reading and thinking? Read the content critically. Does the information present more than one point of view? If not, where else can you look to get alternative perspectives?

› Is the information on the site up to date? For online sources, the date of publication or update can often be found at the top of the article or bottom of the webpage. You can also filter your search results by looking only for pages published within a certain date range.

› Does the author list original data or sources? If online and hyperlinks don't exist or are broken then it may be a sign the information you are reading is out of date or not based on any scholarship, only the author's own ideas.

Listen to a multiplicity of voices as sources. When students are exposed to multiple opinions and ideas about an issue, they can examine different perspectives before constructing their own meaning. When students do this, they learn to triangulate information and not accept just one voice as the only truth. It is also important to determine whose voice is not heard and, when possible, actively seek out sources to uncover those missing voices. Oral history sources often provide those other voices and interpretations. For example, grade 5 students investigating Indigenous people invited a guest speaker from the Anishinabe nation, Phil Cote, to provide an introduction to some Anishinabe rituals, like the smudging ceremony. He sang songs with the students and shared traditional instruments carved with artistic renditions of sacred animals. Spending time with someone from the Anishinabe culture provided a good base for understanding some of their sacred ceremonies.

Frontload concepts. While it is important for students to learn how to conduct effective research, sometimes they spend so much time gathering facts from books and websites that they run out of time to really think about the big ideas and issues. Teachers need to allow time for students to explore unit concepts and to provide support as students develop thinking skills. One way to do this is to provide students with much of the necessary background information (rather than having them discover it). For example, in a grade 5 unit, teachers determined that they would focus on the concept of sustainability. At the start of the unit, the teachers invited the entire grade to a mock Town Hall meeting. The students took on the role of citizens of Bryte City. One teacher, acting as mayor, delivered a presentation about how the town would soon be unable to meet its growing energy demands and needed to determine how best to produce a sustainable electricity source for the future. The other grade 5 teachers role-played a panel of experts and shared information advocating different forms of electricity production. At the end of the meeting, the "mayor" asked students to create a proposal for the Town Council about how to best generate electricity for the city. Over the next couple of weeks, teachers provided

Agenda

- Mayor's welcome
- Electricity shortage information
- Possible solutions
- Q & A

Possible Solutions

- Coal and oil burning electrical station
- Nuclear electrical generating station
- Hydroelectric dam
- Wind farm
- Geothermal heating plant
- Decrease demand, not build a new generator

Powerpoint slides

students with information about how electricity can be generated. Students then used print and online tools to research the pros and cons of different methods of electricity production. Students supported their chosen method of electricity production in a debate. Learning facts about electricity production was not the end goal. The concept of sustainability, as well as the development of research and presentation skills, could now be transferred to other content areas.

Gather your own data from hands-on experiences. Science experiments seem like a natural fit for making observations and gathering data. In kindergarten, students planted bean seeds to determine how they grew. Each day, they observed their seed and documented its progress with a photograph. They uploaded the daily photo to an iPad app that allowed them to add a voiceover describing how their plant looked that day, as well as a prediction about what might happen next. After doing this for a couple of weeks, the students exported all their images, observations, and predictions as one continuous movie that showed the changes that occurred over time. In another class, to chart the growth of the plants, students measured the height of their plant using strips of paper and glued each strip side-by-side to create a bar graph showing growth over time. Through original research, each student gathered primary source knowledge on how plants grow and change over time. Their varied findings could now be used in class discussions about what plants need to survive.

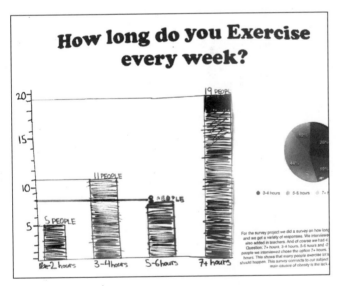

Students researching obesity learned lack of exercise was a common risk factor. They surveyed community members to collect data about their exercise habits.

Take a field trip to learn how something works. Workshops or lessons outside the school can be organized to explore how the world works. For example, grade 4 students learning about different methods of communication attended a workshop about filmmaking. They took on the roles of actors, directors, sound engineers, and camera operators to create their own film. Rather than reading about these roles, students learned about the steps involved in this process through hands-on experience. The experts provided more up-to-date and responsive information than would be found in a text, and students walked away with their own sense of how it felt to go through the

Field trips offer a fun, hands-on way to learn the skills of a discipline.

filmmaking process. Immersion into the world of film equipped students with knowledge about this genre and generated deep questions about how best to tell a story.

Interview people. Interviewing people can lead to a deeper understanding of their thoughts, motivations, and emotions. For grade 3 students, interviewing relatives about how their family came to live in Toronto helped to make their personal histories come alive. Grade 6 students, learning about different ages and stages of life, visited seniors on several occasions, and in the course of their discussions and interviews, learned what it was like to be a young adult in the 1930s and 1940s. Exposing students to a wide range of experiences and life stories can spur further questions to investigate.

Analyze primary documents. One Bold School goal is for students to learn to be scientists, historians, and other kinds of researchers who make their own observations, discuss their findings, and draw their own conclusions. Therefore, we need to create opportunities for students to interact with primary documents that have not already been synthesized by others in textbooks or reports. The use of diaries, census data, letters, speeches, newspapers, and so on can tell a personal story about the past. For example, students in grade 8 referred to primary documents to get a sense of what life was like from 1850 to 1890. They analyzed editorial cartoons to understand different views on Canadian Confederation. Accessing primary documents allowed students to use their thinking skills in critical and creative ways. After reading the primary documents, students drew their own conclusions about whether Canada should have remained sovereign or annexed to the United States. Students communicated their ideas in their own cartoons to demonstrate their understanding and empathy for the issues of that time.

Assessment and Reflection Ideas

Throughout a unit, teachers who focus on inquiry constantly assess students' understanding and skill mastery to determine the progress they are making. This formative assessment allows teachers to identify misunderstandings as they occur and to plan subsequent lessons to clear up misconceptions. We do not want to get to the end of a unit and then realize students misunderstood something back in week

Title: _____   Author: _____

Pourquoi Tales

Criteria	1	2	3	4
Story Elements	- limited story elements present	- some story elements were present (beginning, middle, end)	- many story elements were present (beginning, middle, end)	- well developed beginning, middle and end
Descriptive Details	- Writing shows minimal focus on topic	- Topic is not developed, or focus wanders	- Writing is focused on the topic and has effective story details	- Topic is well developed and has compelling story details
Sentence Structure	- Vocabulary is limited and sentences are simple - limited descriptive phrases	- Writing shows some grade-level vocabulary and/or simple sentence structure - Some effective description	- Writing shows many examples of grade-level vocabulary and sentence structure - Uses descriptive language in many instances	- Writing consistently uses grade-level vocabulary and sentence structure - Uses descriptive language consistently
Process	- jot notes in outlines are limited - created drafts for conferencing - did not effectively use teacher feedback to make revisions	- some jot notes in outlines - included some details in drafts for conferencing - sometimes used teacher feedback to make revisions	- concise jot notes in outlines - created detailed drafts for conferencing - used teacher feedback to make revisions	-crafted concise jot notes in outlines - consistently created detailed drafts for conferencing - effectively used teacher feedback to make revisions

Students conferred with teachers to get feedback on different aspects of their writing.

three. Formative assessment can be conducted formally or informally at multiple stages of the investigation. Teachers determine and record student skill mastery or conceptual understanding by conferring with students, recording anecdotal notes based on observations or conversations, taking photos to document skills, having students reflect on their work in writing, or by recording audio or video reflections. Commercial learning maps like QUIO and Edusight can help both teachers and students be mindful of where they are in the learning process and document levels of proficiency or understanding.

OH SNAP! *Nothing is ever finished; always reflecting and revising*

Since asking questions and developing a research practice represents a key phase of inquiry, it is important to schedule enough class time to ensure deep thinking and understanding of the issues. Students need to understand the research process does not go from A to B; rather, it is iterative. Learning is messy, and you often have to go back, review older research, formulate new questions, and reframe your work. As teachers, we can help students clear up misconceptions and move forward by developing additional provocations to keep the research focused on issues and concepts.

---

6 / DEEPENING INQUIRY: TEACHERS, TECHNOLOGY, AND SMALL GROUPS

What It Is

Classroom teachers can incorporate technology and involve more people from outside the classroom to provide feedback and deepen inquiry. Some schools use a learning commons model to embed additional teacher and digital support within classrooms. A learning commons consists of teacher-librarians, learning-strategies faculty, and technology teachers coordinating with classroom teachers. Communicating and collaborating with teachers in a learning commons provides small groups of students with individualized instruction and ongoing feedback. This, in turn, deepens inquiry.

Why It Is Important for Inquiry

Using the technological and human resources available within schools allows for greater individualization. When teachers collaborate with learning-strategies, technology, and library departments, they create opportunities to work with specialists on small-group work and personalized learning. By working with small groups rather than the whole class at once, teachers are better able to focus work in a student's zone of proximal development and nudge understanding to the next level. Often, the classroom teacher is called on to be the expert in all things, but we may not always know how to do things like blog, curate the current age-appropriate resources at a range of reading levels, and differentiate lessons. Working in smaller groups with more specialized teacher input and feedback enhances the inquiry process. Often, using digital tools can help students get feedback more quickly. There is more time for questions to be answered and refined, and to confer with students at all stages of the investigation.

IT'S ABOUT THE TASK, NOT THE TOOL

Remember that even with the addition of more people and technology, the task should be the focus and the technology used as a tool to facilitate thinking. The expectations need to be the priority rather than the software we use to illustrate these bigger ideas. For example, only teach a particular piece of software or app if it can help students develop or demonstrate their understanding of concepts, knowledge, and skills.

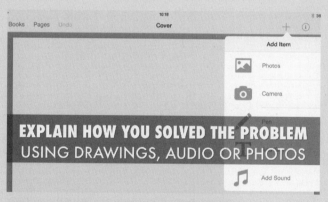

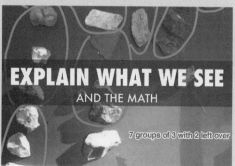

Students used manipulatives to solve math problems and took photographs to document their solution. They annotated the images to explain how they solved the problem. The purpose of using technology was to document what they did and make their thinking visible, not to learn to use specific applications.

Vision

What can this process look like? Students in a Bold School support their points of view with evidence. This can be practised in the research process but also during any class discussions. At this stage of inquiry, there are other adults, in addition to the main teacher, in the classroom to facilitate deeper inquiry through joint lesson planning, team-teaching, and small-group support. This team can provide input on where to find appropriate resources and assistive technologies to help with learning, how to conduct online research, and ways to support both students and teachers throughout the inquiry process. Best-case scenario, classroom teachers have time to coordinate with support teachers to reduce teacher-to-student ratios and promote small-group work.

Challenge

There are many obstacles to creating a classroom that caters to the needs of individual learners. Finding time to organize and provide personalized support can be challenging.

What Steps Can You Take to Make Inquiry Happen for Your Students?

Be flexible when creating small groups for collaboration: change groups from unit to unit or even within a unit, based upon research interest, tasks to be completed, or skill level. Enlist support teachers to help plan for differentiation, promote more active participation through small-group discussion, work with small groups, confer with students, provide feedback or direction to students, or help students understand their possible next steps.

Don't Be Digitally Naïve

It is important to teach digital citizenship skills. Many of us live our lives online. We communicate with family and friends; we check maps and transit schedules, traffic or news updates; we research everything from restaurants to teaching practices; we are entertained; we learn new skills by watching videos or joining courses; and much more. As educators, we often find ourselves trying to prepare students for jobs that might not even exist when they graduate. Who knew ten years ago that children could grow up to work at Shopify or become a website developer? Technology has shifted who has access to knowledge and, in turn, is beginning to change the nature of schools and education. Students are comfortable with technology and are more open to using it than are many of their parents or teachers, but this does not make students experts in learning how to learn digitally.

Enter teachers. Technology offers powerful and engaging tools that can assist with many aspects of inquiry and skill development. Educators need to stay on top of the skills that should be taught in the ever-changing digital environment and determine a plan for all teachers in a school to own part of the teaching of digital citizenship. Students need to be taught and given time to practise everything from how to formally communicate online, to how to access videos, to how to organize their files and folders.

Responsible Digital Citizenship - Safe and ethical behaviour is as important in online environments and communities as it is in the "real world".	
Search for and use images that are not limited by copyright	Utilize copyright-friendly sites Be aware of Creative Commons licensing Understand tools to conduct Advanced Searches
Avoid plagiarism	Cite sources used according to model provided by teacher
Make good decisions regarding their online behaviour	Adhere to website/ app Terms and Conditions Contact a trusted adult if uncomfortable Be able to recognize and respond to cyberbullying Utilize mass emailing appropriately Be able to recognize and respond to online advertising
Understand issues regarding digital identity	Practice online safety Be aware of permanence of digital footprint

Teachers planned what it means to be a good digital citizen in the lower grades. As with other behavioural agreements, the best outcomes are achieved when all faculty model and teach these skills.

Develop digital literacy. Books are valuable, and students should learn to use them to access information. But students also need to learn to navigate content available online. Reading online requires a different skill set than reading paper texts. We need to explicitly teach how to navigate the web so deep reading can occur. For example, students need strategies to know when to click on a hyperlink to glean deeper information on a topic and when to stay on an existing page. The skill set of digital knowledge is too big for one department to own. The teaching of these skills is often woven into library, technology, or subject-specific classes. Technology skills (such as how to navigate the web and discern online bias) is best taught in context rather than in isolation. Effective online research can be problematic for students if specific, explicit skills are not taught. Students need to know how and where to take notes while reading online, how to keep track of specific websites, and how to document sources.

Think critically about sources. The number-one issue students face is confirming the validity of their information sources online. Classroom teachers need to find ways to collaborate with technology teachers and librarians to provide resources for students to think critically and to effectively question the information they find online. Please refer to page 64 for a list of strategies to evaluate electronic resources.

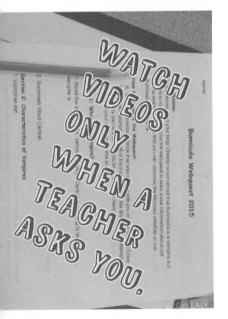

Avoid Digital Distractions

For all of the options for consumption and creation that technology affords, it can also distract some students from completing their work. Time needs to be spent teaching students about how to cope with distraction on the screen. Limiting applications available during school can help. Some students use one username and password to access school files and a separate one to access their personal games and entertainment. This approach of

At the beginning of the year, students determined agreements about appropriate technology use in their classroom together with their teacher. When they started to bend the rules, the teacher decided to have them create and post reminders for their classmates about the agreements.

separating "church and state" is one way to limit distractions. Students are also encouraged to reduce the number of windows open or to use applications like web browser readers so advertising is not visible together with the text they need to read. Timers can help students take breaks from their technology; set a gong or a bell to go off so students know that is time to take a movement and eye break.

Use Your Digital Tools

Every classroom has some students who regularly share their ideas and volunteer information. Yet, for a variety of reasons, there are also some students who rarely speak out in large-group activities. Technology can make it easier for reluctant students to share their ideas.

Don't let writing challenges get in the way of students sharing their ideas.
Writing thoughts and ideas coherently taxes the working memory. Organizing the thoughts in their heads, controlling what their hands are writing, and adhering to spelling and grammar conventions can all present a huge cognitive load on students' brains. For some students, using technology such as audio or video tools instead of writing by hand to record their ideas allows them to provide more detail and to more accurately reflect on their learning.

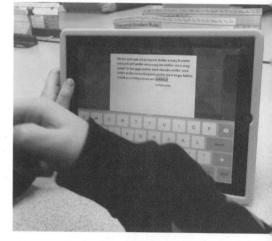

This grade 2 student used the word prediction feature to accurately spell challenging words while working on a weekly letter to parents.

For example, when Carly Crippin's grade 3 students used Apple's Photobooth to record their end-of-unit reflections, she noticed a greater level of detail was communicated than when they documented their ideas in writing. Audio or video recordings are now easy to create with computers, tablets, or mobile phones. These digital tools are effective ways for students to show what they know without writing down all their ideas. Students with reading and writing challenges can use assistive technologies that turn voice into text or text into voice.

Some classroom teachers schedule mini-lessons with the teacher-librarian, learning-strategies teacher, or technology teachers to support research. Pam Love and Adrienne Fisher, our librarians, recommend online encyclopaedias, such as PebbleGo, that can read text aloud to students. Students enjoy using text-to-speech technology for research to access challenging texts about the brain, European explorers, and animal adaptations, for example. Such technology also helps students with reading difficulties access content without the need for adult assistance. Library periods can be used to facilitate small-group work, or additional time can be scheduled whenever support teachers are available to help in the classroom.

Hear all voices. Rather than just one person being able to give a response at a time, electronic discussions through learning management systems or email allow all students to have a voice. Online tools such as Padlet, Socrative, or Kahoot can be used for brainstorming or to conduct polls that allow all students to share their ideas.

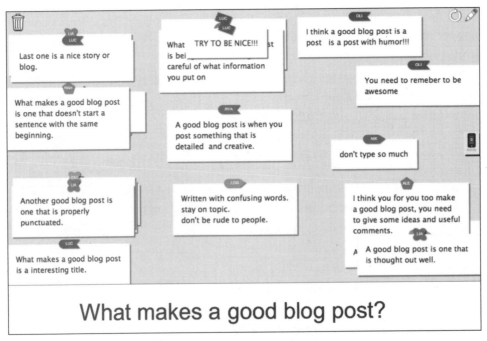

Students explored blog posts written by students at another school. They then shared their ideas about what makes a good blog post using a digital sticky note application. A class discussion categorizing the comments followed before students wrote their own blog posts.

These tools let all students answer teacher-generated questions at the same time. Teachers can select the tools that best meet their needs and easily keep track of levels of participation.

Work on one product together. It is still important to learn to write by hand and to read handwriting. However, technology affords the possibility of new learning engagements not possible with pencil and paper. Online tools, such as Pirate Pad or Google Documents, allow multiple writers to work on one electronic document simultaneously. Working together on one product helps students and teachers learn from one another and build on one another's ideas. Students can study independently or in small groups and then combine and share their work in common spaces to create one class project.

For example, in a unit about finite resources and sharing the planet, grade 6 students at The York School became passionate about reducing the amount of plastic that ends up as waste in landfills. They made a documentary film as part of their larger campaign to ban plastic bags. Creating a documentary is not often part of grade 6 classroom practice, but technology allowed students to play many different roles in the research, production, and editing processes and meet expectations in several subject areas.

Free up time to collaborate using analogue tools. Paradoxically, using technology can help teachers find more time in class for nontechnology-related activities. Traditionally, teachers lectured in classrooms, and then students went home and worked on practice problems. In the flipped-classroom model, students learn about different concepts for homework and then work on problems in class together with the teacher. In this model, content required for homework is often delivered electronically via readings or videos, which may already be available online or created by teachers. For example, physics teacher Reed Jeffrey created his own physics videos on YouTube, and if students had questions, they were encouraged to post them in a shared space. The next day, Jeffrey addressed the questions at the start of class as part of the discussion time. Some of the benefits of this model included more time in class to work through challenging problems with guidance and to clear up misconceptions about the content. In this case, the technology used at home allowed for more inquiry and collaboration to happen in the classroom through hands-on experiments.

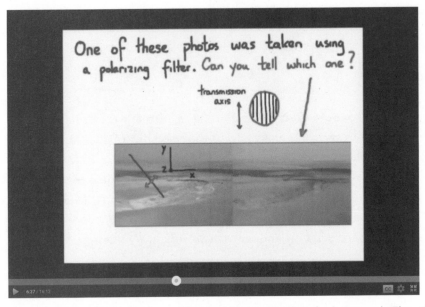

One of these photos was taken using a polarizing filter. Can you tell which one?

transmission axis

Students reviewed videos about different physics concepts for homework. They then came to class with questions and some background information. This led to deeper discussions and more time in class to work on experiments.

Create a digital learning community. Digital experts like Alan November (2012b) suggest assigning different roles to students during lectures and teacher-led discussions to enrich the learning experience through active learning. He advocates that, as a regular course of events in the classroom, students be assigned or sign up for roles within their learning community as they study a particular topic. Roles could include the following: Tutorial Designer, develops review materials to consolidate learning; Scribe, takes notes that will be shared with all; Researcher, answers searchable questions on the fly; Global Communicator/Collaborator, contacts any experts and conduct interviews. November devised these roles as part of the "digital farm." Years ago, children made meaningful contributions through farmwork. Now, these roles allow students to make meaningful contributions to classroom learning. Technology allows all of this work to be shared with the class or to be done collaboratively by a group of students. These communities can be located within one classroom, within a school, or globally.

Expand your digital learning community to include social media. These types of tools provide personal reports of life from around the world. Alan November described how a teacher used Twitter hashtags to obtain local commentary on the 2011 Egyptian Revolution. After participating in a conversation on Twitter, he made arrangements for his students to participate in a Skype call with a woman in Cairo to gain a firsthand account of daily life in Egypt and the events in Tahrir Square in particular.

DEVELOP ONLINE SEARCH SKILLS

Eli Pariser, CEO of Upworthy, describes a "filter bubble" in which search engines use algorithms to bring results tailored to users based on past queries. In the future, when users search, the results most similar to those previously clicked on are returned first, and users see more of what is already familiar to them. According to Pariser, "the Internet is showing us what it thinks we want to see but not necessarily what we need to see" (2011). We want to avoid this to expand our perspective on issues.

Students benefit from knowing how to search the web in a precise and efficient manner. Teachers can consider teaching the following search skills:

› Using quotation marks around text forces the search engine to look for that exact phrase.

› Using a dash or minus sign excludes some terms from search results.

› Accessing Google through different country addresses yields different results. For example, going to google.ca (Google Canada) and looking for information on a current event will provide different responses than searching for the same event in the United Kingdom at google.co.uk (or from any other country code).

› Searching in incognito mode or using search engines like DuckDuckGo prevents websites you previously searched from being tracked. In Google Chrome, for example, if users right click on the New Tab menu, they can open a new tab or window in incognito mode and escape their filter bubble.

Provide Feedback

There are several ways teachers can provide scaffolding and nudge learning. A benefit of working in small groups is the frequent feedback offered. Immediate and specific feedback to students enables them to make refinements and adjustments. Find ways to create small groups by inviting other teachers into the classroom to free up time for personalized support.

Use questions to elicit feedback. Discuss any aspect of the learning process and/or the product students are creating. Coaching expert Ian Chisholm (2014) asks students of all ages three questions to elicit feedback: What was good? What was tricky? What would you do differently? Picking one of these questions can start a productive conversation. Conversations that result from the answers to these questions can facilitate metacognition or thinking about thinking. When teachers discuss different aspects of the process, as well as the product, students can adjust and tackle problems based on specific feedback.

Ask administrators for preservice teachers. Students enrolled in a teaching program often provide a fresh set of eyes for extra practice, review, and feedback while completing their practicum at schools. Student teachers often come armed with the latest research and insights on teaching and learning. Interactive whiteboards suddenly get turned on and the manipulatives for math come out of the cupboard when student teachers are allowed to plan lessons.

For example, to launch a unit about European explorers, student teachers dressed up and adopted roles as monarchs from Spain, France, England, and Portugal, then challenged students to write a successful application to become a royal explorer. The addition of drama and pageantry drew the students into the unit and helped them understand and explain some of the key character traits of explorers. More teachers in the room facilitated the writing process.

GOALS	STRATEGIES FOR ACHIEVING GOALS
1. Research and implement the use of assistive technology devices to help boys with written output	-Research assistive technology to determine best fit -Plan how-to lessons with individual boys and the whole class to help them use the devices to improve their written output -Monitor the students to ensure that devices are beneficial for learning and completing classroom assignments
2. Develop my instructional strategies in math to support my extension group	-Plan and implement hands-on, fun lessons based on brain research to support and foster students math skills and understanding -Develop my own positive disposition towards math, as a way to transfer enthusiasm to my students -Become more confident and comfortable teaching this subject area

Student teachers worked with the host teacher to set goals for the practicum. Learning how to differentiate instruction and implement technology are often key priorities for new teachers. Development of these areas also benefit the school.

Independent work facilitates the running of small groups. When a teacher wants to work with a small group to teach a reading strategy or to provide extra practice in a recently taught concept, for example, the rest of the class usually completes independent work comprising one or a number of tasks. Such independent work should allow the teacher an uninterrupted block of time of at least 20 minutes in which to work with the small group. Students engaged in independent work do not all have to be working in the same subject area: some students might finish up a writing assignment while others practise a previously taught math concept. Sometimes, a teacher can simply give the rest of the class time for independent reading while he or she works directly with the small group to provide feedback.

Call on other adults to help run a group. Often there are many other adults in our families, schools, and communities who are willing to help teachers. We need to build systems and strategies so adults who are not necessarily teachers, but who have knowledge and skill, can regularly bring their gifts into the classroom. Send an email or a put out a call on the PA system to find adults to help a small group practise reading a transit map to plan for a field trip. Parents can sign up to read aloud to children in the primary grades.

Schedule more teachers during high-impact periods. Work with administration to enlist other teachers to help during high-impact inquiry periods. Additional support staff improve the teacher-student ratio for these learning groups. At our school, administrators schedule student teachers and teaching assistants to be in classrooms during the morning inquiry block to help run experiments and centres, to field student questions, and to document learning during science and social studies inquiry time. We also schedule available teachers who have literacy teaching expertise to teach and push questioning during guided reading groups. This approach provides multiple groups to run simultaneously with support. This way, more students receive direct feedback and teaching on their reading skills. Personalized learning flourished three mornings a week with this timetable innovation. When administration provides dedicated time for a team of teachers to individualize instruction and deepen inquiry in the classroom, it realizes its goals of making authentic inquiry a reality.

CONFERRING EFFECTIVELY WITH STUDENTS

If teachers can help students refine their questions, students will have a better understanding of the types of questions that require further exploration. Students in small groups have more opportunity to pursue their own questions with teacher guidance, and the teacher can cater to different learning styles.

› Have a small group of students confer with a teacher for an extended period of time (even as short as twenty minutes) whenever possible. Students will benefit from this more individualized approach.

› The small-group format enables teachers to provide not only feedback but individualized attention. Teachers working with two or more students can provide ongoing feedback to help students deepen their understanding of the skill or concept they are learning.

› Mastering conceptual understanding is often easier to achieve in a small-group context. Students can get answers to their questions, and teachers can instruct through different modalities, depending on the learners.

› Establishing a process whereby a teacher provides counsel and a student revises work before receiving additional direction allows for low-stakes practice and more individualized learning.

Extend Reach

There are many experts available who can help with student research about challenging topics and concepts. Mine the experts in your school and community to help both teachers and students.

Connect students with professionals to learn more about issues. When you engage experts to teach lessons in class, answer student questions, or act as sounding boards for students' ideas about issues, students gain a deeper understanding of the core questions of a discipline. Engineers can offer information, resources, and real-life examples on a simple machines unit, for example. Filmmakers can teach aspects of the media literacy curriculum with examples from the field to potentially inspire projects for further study. Outside agencies and organizations are often keen to provide information on topics within their range of expertise. For example, students studying how masculinity is defined in North American advertisements might seek feedback from creatives in the advertising industry or from an organization like Parents, Families, and Friends of Lesbians and Gays (PFLAG). When experts provide students with meaningful feedback, students are engaged in the big questions of the discipline.

Engage students as experts. Students are usually eager to share their personal experiences with others, and technology has made it easy for them to connect with others around the world. For example, in a unit about celebrations, Pina Porto's kindergarten students came across a Mexican holiday about which they knew little. None of the books in the school library described this celebration. Since the teachers couldn't find any resources available at a five-year-old reading level, they decided to conduct a video call with a grade 2 classroom at an English-speaking international school in Mexico to ask about the holiday and how they celebrated it. Participating in this type of discussion helped to teach communication skills and also provided answers to the students' questions. They were able to do their research by talking to other students who were "experts" in the subject matter.

Recruit older students as mentors. Sometimes students benefit from feedback from older students who have been through a similar academic experience. Older students can be reading buddies with younger readers. This way, younger readers can hear what fluent readers do: attend to punctuation, read with expression, and use proper phrasing. They can also ask their buddy questions about the content of their reading and work together on a special project, which models reading for a purpose. For example, grade 1 and grade 3 reading buddies reflected on the book *You Are Stardust* by Elin Kelsey and worked on a gratitude project for Earth Day. Each pair brainstormed what they were thankful for and presented their ideas and statements at the assembly. These types of interactions can create empathy among learners.

Peer tutors and research buddies can reteach subject matter and run small groups. The use of research buddies can involve pairing up older students to assist younger students throughout the various steps of the research process. For example, grade 3 classes working on animal adaptation reports paired up with grade 7 students (many of whom had done similar reports previously). The older students helped the younger ones locate and analyze information and make jot notes to deepen understanding of content.

Feedback to our Students:

Feel free to comment on the following areas of the debate performance on the feedback form.

- Ability to make an effective argument (i.e. include a topic sentence, supporting details and concluding sentence)

- Uses evidence to back up argument (i.e. statistics, data)

- Asks a point of information in a concise way

- Refutes the arguments of the other team

- Speaks clearly with good pacing and expression

- Makes eye contact with the judges and members of the audience

- Uses time allotted effectively

Judges used this checklist to structure feedback to middle-school debaters to help them prepare for their next debate. Templates like this can also help peer tutors focus on learning goals.

Many schools run formal tutoring programs. Older students, often in high school, can sign up to regularly work with younger students in one of their academic areas of strength. Typically some training is provided for the peer tutors on how to work with younger students, including how to break skills down and how to assist with general organization and support executive functioning skill development. We have several, older students connected to our after-school homework program. Once a week, they work with younger students on a range of academic subjects. We often call on them for math support. Students who already know how to multiply and divide, for example, can help those who are not yet proficient practise and consolidate these skills. Boarding students from Quebec who are native French speakers help younger students master components of the French language. The benefit of these types of groups work on several levels. There are advantages not only to the tutee, but to the tutor, who shares knowledge and understanding. There is also a social element at play as the students exchange information about the expectations and routines of future grades. These types of interactions provide reassurance and a sense of calm about the future.

Assessment and Reflection Ideas

Formative assessment is key to developing mastery of skills, and building practice time into the schedule is one way to make this happen. All teacher observations can help determine a student's strengths and the next step in the learning process. Several teachers working with your students, taking notes, and recording class discussions can help determine trends and next steps. Provide standardized forms to other teachers and adults who work with your students to record any student questions or document growth to facilitate the collection of information.

Name_____

3J READING CONFERENCE

READS		STRATEGIES				COMPREHENSION						LITERARY ELEMENTS								LEVEL			
Fluently	Word by Word	Sounds Words	Pictorial/ Layout Context Clues	Syntax Clues	Self-Corrects	Uses Prior Knowledge	Predicts	Infers	Supports w/Text	Thinks Critically	Genre	Plot	Setting	Characters	Author/ Illustrator	Style/Theme/ Mood	Text Form	Content	Accuracy	Too Easy	Appropriate	Too Hard	Reads Independently

Date:
Book Title:
Comments:

Date:
Book Title:
Comments:

Date:
Book Title:
Comments:

	Text:	
Questioning • Ask critical-thinking questions before, during or after reading • Use questions to clarify thinking	Text:	
Monitoring Comprehension • Take action in flexible ways to solve problems or fit purpose to genre • Check on accuracy and understanding and work to self-correct errors. • thinking aloud • Self-correction	Text:	
Evaluating • Think critically about the text • judge, justify, or defend understandings; • use of evidence from text to support opinion	Text:	
Synthesizing • Adjust present understandings to accommodate new knowledge. • merging new info from the text, with current knowledge to create new understandings, ideas or opinions	Text:	
Visualizing • make a mental picture so that you can comprehend what the author is saying • draw a picture on paper to aide comprehension	Text:	
Prior Knowledge • discuss students' prior knowledge of and about content of the text; • prior knowledge of the text's format	Text:	
Analyze • Notice aspects of the writer's craft and text structure	Text:	

These templates were used to keep track of student reading development. Teachers conferred with students during silent-reading blocks to discuss what they were reading, practice a skill, and recommend new books. They also recorded observations during guided-reading blocks to plan future sessions.

This rubric shows how students were assessed on how they explained their mathematical thinking. While having the correct answer was important, being able to explain the strategy they used and how they double-checked their answer were also vital.

"Explain Your Thinking" Rubric

	Answer	Strategy	Checked
4	I wrote the correct answer in a complete sentence.	I described all the steps in my strategy using pictures or numbers **AND** words.	I checked that my answer makes sense.
3	I wrote the correct answer but it was not in a complete sentence.	I used pictures or numbers **AND** words to describe my strategy but I left out some steps.	I checked that my answer makes sense but I made the same mistake again.
2	I did not write the correct answer but I used a complete sentence.	I described a strategy that does not make sense although it may have the correct answer.	When I checked, I got a different answer but I didn't change anything.
1	I did not write any sentence with my answer.	I did not try to explain my strategy or my explanation does not make sense.	I did not check my answer.

Date:

Author's name:

Title of work:

Peer Conference

Reviewer's name:

Text Structure

Writing has a strong beginning	☺	😐	☹
Writing has an entertaining or informative middle	☺	😐	☹
Writing has a satisfying ending	☺	😐	☹

Language Features

Writing has information that describes the main ideas	☺	😐	☹
Writing uses interesting and descriptive words	☺	😐	☹
Writing has different sentence patterns	☺	😐	☹
There is a mixture of action, description, dialogue or topics	☺	😐	☹

My partner liked

My partner suggested that I

Self-edit

Mechanics			
Capitalization: Capital letters are used correctly for names, places, dates and the beginning of sentences	☺	😐	☹
Omissions: Words are not missing from the sentences	☺	😐	☹
Punctuation: Punctuation is used correctly at the end of every sentence	☺	😐	☹
Spelling: Grade level words are spelled correctly	☺	😐	☹

After reading multiple examples of stories, students, with their teacher, determined the criteria for a good story. After they drafted their own story, students read their work aloud to a partner who provided feedback about structure and language usage. Students edited their own work and were expected to take their partners' feedback into consideration when revising their drafts.

Students photograph the work they do, using an iPad. They then describe what they were learning and share these digital portfolios with their parents at student-led conferences.

E-portfolios are a good way to capture student growth over time. Students as young as kindergarten can take photographs or video of their work and annotate the images with text or audio. Voice-to-text features allow even young students to add text to a page before knowing how to type or spell.

WHAT IT LOOKS LIKE IN THE CLASSROOM – RESEARCH IN ACTION

In the International Baccalaureate Diploma Programme, students undertake an extended essay project meant to prepare them for undergraduate research. Students select a topic of interest related to one of the subjects they are studying. They then analyze, synthesize, and evaluate knowledge before presenting an argument in "an independent, self-directed piece of research, finishing with a 4,000-word paper" (IBO 2015).

At our school, students undertake the extended essay in grade 11. Librarian Mari Roughneen, Learning Strategist Jody McLean, and Curriculum Coordinator Julia Kinnear examined the feedback they had received in previous years from teachers, students, and the International Baccalaureate (the external grading institution). With that feedback, they worked together to determine how to scaffold this challenging project for students.

They faced two key challenges: how to teach all applicants the process for engaging in the work and how to communicate common messages to all stakeholders in the project (students, advisors, and parents) without dedicated class time. To improve communication, teachers used online tools to organize resources and provide tips to support students as they worked on their own. The learning commons team delivered workshops to scaffold the process and to make the challenging essay-writing process fun while still using best practices. To do this, they held an Intellectual Spirit Week that highlighted the research process, potential pitfalls, and various resources to help them navigate the task. Through video reflections, students and teachers who had already been through the process shared struggles, celebrated victories, and provided advice for those now doing the project.

As students presented their essay proposals, the librarian provided workshops on information literacy, research, the structure of academic thesis papers, and resources available in the community to help the students with their particular topic. The curriculum coordinator taught the learning skills students needed to develop throughout this project (communication, social, self-management, research, and critical thinking). The learning strategist helped develop timelines. The process was chunked to keep students on track: clear timelines were developed for when students should select their subject, be assigned a supervisor, participate in workshops, complete their draft, revise, and submit their final paper. This team of teachers taught students to view themselves as researchers and referred students to particular resources (including experts and other students).

The librarian, learning strategist, and curriculum coordinator met regularly to reflect on what was working well and to discuss the types of challenges the students encountered. Through regular communication of student progress, this group effectively and efficiently developed targeted plans to keep the essays on topic and on schedule, and focused on inquiry.

OH SNAP *Nothing is ever finished; always reflecting and revising*

Student self-management is crucial to making small-group work successful within the confines of a whole class. Students need to learn how to work independently when their teachers are conferring with other students. Ideally, we find time to teach our students habits of mind, perseverance, and self-regulation so they become effective independent learners. If we spend time teaching these learning-how-to-learn skills, it frees us up to provide more personalized support for small groups.

Collaboration requires a lot of effort and time. Time is needed for support teachers to regularly communicate with one another and other faculty to provide a consistent and coherent approach.

7 / HOW MIGHT WE USE WHAT WE HAVE LEARNED TO CONTRIBUTE TO OUR LIVES OR THE LIVES OF OTHERS?

What It Is

Students need time to reflect on what they have learned and consider how it might be used to make a difference in their lives or the lives of others. Teachers debrief with students to process their new learning and engage their thinking skills. Divergent thinking figures prominently at this stage, as students imagine a number of possibilities about who could benefit from their new learning in the local or global community.

When students engage their divergent thinking skills they:

›   Think critically. Students look at issues from multiple points of view before developing their own point of view. At this stage, critical thinking includes processing and reflecting on new knowledge.

›   Think compassionately. Find ways for students to connect with different audiences and communities to develop a sense of concern for others. Once students identify key learnings with teacher support, the group starts to flex their empathy muscles to determine if there is a person, group, or organization that might benefit from their learning.

› Think creatively. Students imagine and brainstorm how to make a difference or a change for ourselves, others, or both. Contributions can be big or small, local or global, but age-appropriate, and within their sphere of influence.

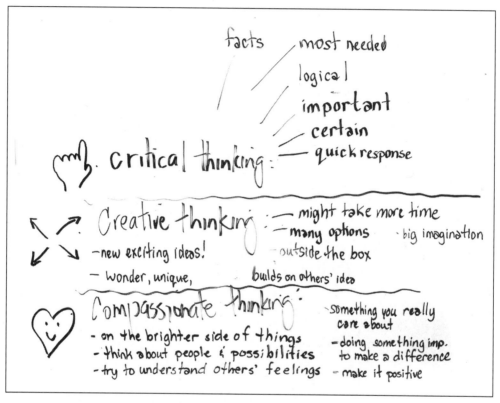

The students brainstormed definitions for the three Cs of thinking.

Why It Is Important for Inquiry

Determining how you might make a difference resonates for all inquirers because it makes the work we do in schools meaningful. Kids can understand at an early age how their knowledge and actions can affect their lives and the lives of others.

Vision

What does this process look like? You might see students highlighting and reviewing their notes to make sense of their inquiry. Other students might be reviewing learning logs of past reflections to gauge how communities or individuals could benefit from their knowledge. Small groups of students might identify organizations that support local community services and agencies, or address current events. Teachers could ask questions to extend divergent thinking and to generate more ideas with the whole class or small groups.

Challenge

Making time to debrief and make connections can be hard to schedule with all of the priorities schools need to juggle.

What Steps Can You Take to Make Inquiry Happen for Your Students?

Teachers can begin by creating empathetic classrooms and ensuring students have a voice. By frequently asking students about how others might perceive situations, we build empathy. We can do this when discussing characters in a story, reading about different community members and their perspectives on issues, and reviewing science on particular theories about the natural world. We need to constantly ask students how their actions might benefit others. Whether issues arise on the playground or decisions need to be made about what to do next in class, when teachers solicit, then implement student ideas, students learn their voices matter and they can actually make a difference.

Schedule Regular Debrief Meetings

Learning new ideas often happens at a quick pace. After teachers introduce a concept, students might not have enough social or individual thinking time to assimilate the new information. There is power in giving students time to reflect and debrief new findings individually, in small groups, or with the entire class. For example, grade

Strategies to stay in control

Forgetting about it and Ignoring It. Tell a adult, change the subject and to take a deep breath and go back to what I'm doing.

KEEP CALM

Strategies to stay in control

Closing my eyes for around 20 seconds and trying to normal-ize my breathing speed.

KEEP CALM AND CARRY ON

Strategies to stay in control

To breath slowly, say positive stuff.

Strategies to stay in control

My strategy to stay incontrol is to take deep breathes and ask my brother to please stop and please don't do it again.

KEEP CALM AND CARRY ON

After a group debrief session, students individually recorded the strategies they would use to stay in control.

3 students learned about the limbic system (their emotional brain) and strategies to calm emotions. Teachers mapped out time to debrief what they had learned about self-regulation with students. During the debrief time, students determined their individual strategies for self-regulation. After they processed their new learning, they could consolidate new information more readily. One student realized if he was in a fight with a peer after a four-square game, he needed to walk away and count to 10 to settle down before talking about the conflict. Scheduling debrief meetings provides intentional time for students to think critically, creatively, and compassionately during the school day.

Develop a Sense of Connection with Other Cultures

Connecting students to different cultures helps to build empathy and promote intercultural awareness. Lisa Fleming's grade 2 class in Toronto, Canada, shared images and text about what they were learning with pen pals from Rhena Bowie's

Places in the School
We should show them!

1) Playground
2) Upper School drive way
3) Outdoor space
4) Field (ice rink, football field etc)
5) Wild things garden
6) Gym
7) Library
8) Learning garden
9) Our Classroom !!!
10) Art room ; big art room
11) Science lab
12) Cubbies
13) Weston Hall
14) Primary office

After viewing a video sent to them by their partner school, students were struck by both the similarities and differences to their own school. Students decided they should make a video tour of the school to send to their pen pals. They brainstormed locations to include on the tour, then broke into small groups to film each part of the tour. The teacher pieced their work together into one movie and shared it with the other school.

grade 1 class in Luanda, Angola, through personal blog posts. Grade 1 students in the Angolan school, halfway around the globe, read and responded to the blog posts. Sharing these conversations also allowed teachers and parents to take part, which often led to conversations about other school cultures and traditions and to a deeper sense of connection. We build student capacity for compassionate thinking when we design these sorts of intercultural experiences for our students.

Expand Your Perspective

Technology allows students to conduct global inquiries by connecting with other classes or experts to gather information. When students research different subtopics and then share vital information with peers who need it to complete another task, their efforts are valued. Students also realize the necessity of providing clear and accurate information. For example, Craig Parkinson's high-school students in Toronto made curriculum connections with a school in Lewa, Kenya. A key goal of the project was to develop a relationship based on a common experience. By conducting the same experiments in each country the two classes learned about their local soil. On a blog, they shared and discussed their findings about percolation rates and moisture retention. As a group, they determined factors that might account for differences between the two countries and the impact of their findings.

From a North American perspective, students were concerned about toxins in the soil, how they would leach through the soil, and where they would end up. The Kenyan students, many of whom came from farming backgrounds, were interested in irrigation and agricultural conditions of the soil. The project achieved subject-specific goals and instilled in the students a sense of mutual appreciation and understanding.

Brainstorm Possibilities for Helping Others

The result of a critical, creative, and compassionate thinking process might lead to multiple ways to make a difference through action or service. A number of low- or high-tech options, such as mind maps, webs, lists, or any other graphic organizers, can be used to visualize information from class discussions. Creating a representation of divergent thinking helps students organize and summarize key information, identify patterns, and determine relationships and trends. With practice, a student can lead a questioning sequence to generate ideas with classmates; the teacher can serve as a scribe. After ideas are generated, students select an action. For example, in grade 5, students had just finished a debate on whether or not to buy local food. After a vigorous debate on the pros and cons, students brainstormed who would benefit from the information they had generated and which stakeholders could make a significant change based on the information. Family members could use this new learning to inform household shopping decisions. The eco-club could communicate the information to a broader audience. Finally, someone suggesting sharing with the parent committee and the kitchen staff. This led them to the kitchen staff. The students presented information about the benefit of buying local foods when the produce was in season, which resulted in changes to the menus based on the availability of local produce. The brainstorming phase generated many ideas, and a culling process helped students arrive at a viable and valuable idea. Students then made an informed decision based on careful thinking.

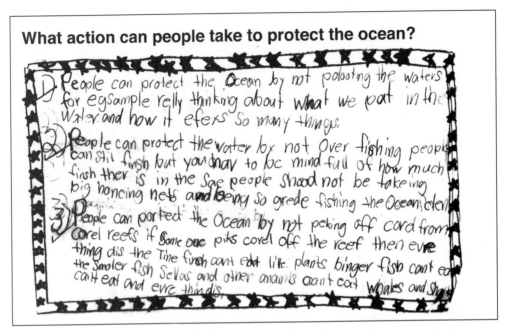

What action can people take to protect the ocean?

1) People can protect the Ocean by not polooting the waters for egsample relly thinking about what we pat in the Water and how it efexs so many thinge.

2) People can protect the water by not over fishing people can stil finsh but you dnav to be mindfull of how much finsh ther is in the Sae people shood not be takeing big honcing nets and being so grede fishing the Ocean olen

3) People can partect the Ocean by not peking off corel from Corel reefs if some one piks corel off the reef then evre thing dis the Tine finsh cant edt like plants binger fish cant eat the Smaler fish Sellas and other anamls cant eat whales and sharks cant eat and evre thin dis.

After inquiring into ocean habitats, students individually brainstormed ways to protect this important resource.

Assessment and Reflection Ideas

Formative assessment continues throughout this phase. Continue to take notes or record class discussions for future use. Keep charts and take photos of whiteboards so each can be revisited during debrief meetings to reflect on and consolidate learning.

OH SNAP! *Nothing is ever finished; always reflecting and revising*

Carve out time in the schedule to regularly debrief learning experiences.

Find ways to build learning and understanding of different communities as potential audiences with which to share learning.

---

8 / WHAT TYPE OF CHANGE PROJECT CAN WE DESIGN FOR A REAL AUDIENCE?

What It Is

With change projects, students and teachers use what they know about an issue to affect real audiences. The goal of conducting a change project is to make a difference based on your learning. The first step in taking action requires students to deeply

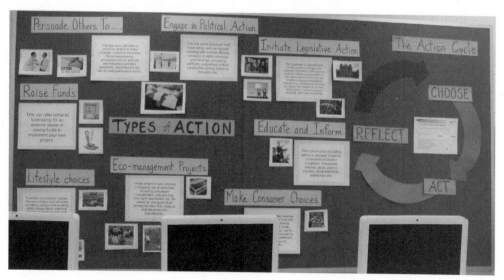

Students are encouraged to take action beyond fundraising. Students can design change projects to educate and inform, change consumer choices, involve political action, initiate legislative action, participate in eco-management projects, and promote healthy lifestyle choices (Burgess 2003).

understand local or global issues. Next, students brainstorm potential stakeholders who are affected by this issue. They then work individually, in a small group, or with a whole class to design a plan for change. At this stage of the inquiry process, convergent thinking kicks in, as students narrow down their options and determine a way to create change from learning.

Why It Is Important for Inquiry

Change projects allow students to demonstrate their critical, creative, and compassionate thinking. This process makes learning authentic, because students engage in meaningful work and share findings with real audiences. The varied ways students can demonstrate their knowledge about an issue with change projects also supports personalized learning.

Students apply skills and knowledge learned in class by engaging in action. This answers the question students have been known to ask on many occasions: "Why do I have to know this?" It allows them to make connections between learning and life outside the classroom and provides motivation for learning new skills and gaining new knowledge.

Some teachers find it helpful to collaborate with other adults in the school community to determine possible ways to take action. For example, a classroom teacher asked kitchen staff to act as consultants after his students had investigated child poverty. The students learned about the different types of lunches people eat globally, depending on their income level and where they live: 13% of children are in chronic hunger, 63% sometimes have enough to eat, and 24% always have enough to eat. The school cook shared the idea of holding a special lunch to simulate both the types and percentages of foods eaten around the world. The students agreed. In consultation with the kitchen staff, the students chose rice and beans, porridge, and a hamburger with pop and dessert to represent foods typically eaten. Students paid five dollars to participate, knowing they would draw one of the three types of lunches. Even though many were game to experiment at the onset, some students did not enjoy the lunch they received (beans and rice, or porridge). Others were grateful to receive the premium lunch option of a hamburger, ice cream, chips, and pop.

Working with several members of the school community to simulate a real-life experience helped students practise a variety of skills. Taking action, in this instance, required students to fulfil many tasks, such as meeting with the kitchen staff to plan meals, designing the menu to present the three different types of lunches, and promote and organize the event to their grade. The students used checklists, research, and expert knowledge to figure out exactly what was needed for the event.

Vision

What does the process look like? Teachers could facilitate whole-class or small-group discussions by asking questions to support convergent thinking. Or they could mentor students as they design their plans. You might see students on the phone booking a meeting to share their learning. Other students design a website to share their information. At this juncture, students collaborate with one another to contribute to the logistics of a project as they determine which group member will contact a particular agency, organize transportation to get to the action site, determine the specific jobs each group member will complete, and so on.

Challenge

Kids often spend a lot of time conducting research or investigating an issue in school and then reporting their findings to the class. Students do not always feel compelled to put forth their best effort if their classroom peers and teacher represent their only audience members. Finding authentic audiences for student learning is one way to motivate students.

Students in grade 5 participated in the lottery lunch.

What Steps Can You Take to Make Inquiry Happen for Your Students?

Teachers can play a huge role in shifting student perspectives to take action beyond traditional fundraising. This shift in thinking, if taught explicitly, can crack open the notion of what it means to serve, and connect to making a meaningful difference through action that is engaging and significant. In sharing their stories, teachers can model how empathy about someone's situation can be transformed into action. Teachers can share anecdotes about change projects that they personally engage in (either within the school community or outside of school) to fuel ideas for students to take personal action or help with class action projects. For example, physical education teacher Kristin Buchanan shared stories with her students about the Habitat for Humanity building projects she participates in over the summer months. As the head of the action committee at her school, she encourages students to engage in their own change projects.

Classroom Change Projects

Even the youngest learners can take action after gathering data. For example, senior-kindergarten students each took an inventory in their home of the polishes, detergents, and liquids used for household cleaning. At school, the students tallied their information to categorize cleaning supplies according to their level of eco-friendliness. Through the inventory process, students noticed the majority of household cleaners contained some level of toxic substances. In response to this data, they created their own brand of eco-friendly household cleaners after conducting research with their teachers on the types of ingredients that would be required. After preparing the cleaners, the students wrote letters to their parents explaining the differences between what was currently used at home and the recommended replacement (made from essential oils, vinegar, and water). Through primary research, teachers helped students understand the risk of using cleaners with chemicals and how their homemade cleaner represented a better choice for the environment. Students came to understand that what you buy can affect your environment.

Survey: What is going down our drains?

Parents, please do a survey of household products WITH your daughter. You will need to write the information carefully in the chart so that she can read it. We need to have the survey returned on Tuesday. Please make sure she understands all the information on the chart (except for the chemical names/column 4) before returning it.

	Product Name (soap, cleaner, toiletry, chemical?)	Where in house do we use it?	Why do we use it? What does it do?	What is in it? (chemical names)	Is it biodegradable? Yes/No
1	avalon organics glycerin hand soap	bathroom	hand+body soap.	aqua, cocamidopropyl betaine, disodium cocoamphodiacetate, sodium cocoyl sarcosinate, cocout, propalkonium chloride, rosemary leaf extract, calendula flower extract, glycerin, chamomile	yes, babassu am, Wild panthe tocopheroli Ethyl hex
2	green beaver natural toothpaste	bathroom Sink	brush teeth	calcium carbonate, sorbitol, aqua, glycerin, aroma, sodium bicarbonate, citrus aurantium dulcis oil, xylitol, silica, peppermint oil,	yes lemon menthol, calcium
3	dermtologica body scrub	tub	body scrub	ascorbate, tea tree, sclerotium gum, coco gl xanthan gum papaya enzymes, rice bran, olive, fig, date, lavendar, orange, sandalwood, rosemary, patchouli	?
4	seabuckthorn shampoo	tub	shampoo clean hair	springwater, herbal infusions in jojoba oil seabuckthorn, calendula, red clover, oats, coltsfoot, horsetail, comfry, nettles, chamomile, seaweed, yucca,	doesn't say prob is. YES
5	ecover dishwashing liquid	kitchen Sink	wash dishes	cocoa-protein, orange wax, rosemary grapefruit, peppermint, vetivert lime essential oils. aqua, sodium lauroth sulfate.	yes.

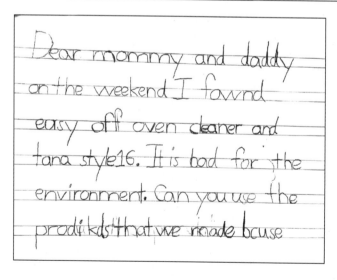

Dear mommy and daddy on the weekend I fawnd easy off oven cleaner and tana style16. It is bad for the environment. Can you use the prodiikdsthat we made bcuse

Senior-kindergarten students examined cleaning products used at home and documented the chemicals that go down drains. After learning about more environmentally friendly cleaners in class, students wrote persuasive letters to their parents in an effort to change their buying habits.

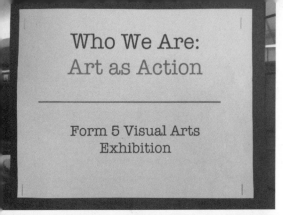

Who We Are:
Art as Action

Form 5 Visual Arts Exhibition

A grade 5 student researched the effects of concussions and how they can be prevented. His artwork attracted much attention from the community and was presented together with more information about sports injuries.

Community Change Projects

Teachers can help students develop change projects to undertake within a community. For example, a grade 5 class investigated accessibility issues. To get a sense of what life can be like for people with a physical disability, they attended school for three days in rented wheelchairs. They gathered data about trouble spots within the school over the course of the experiment. In consultation with their teacher, they booked a meeting with the school's Facilities Director to report on their findings. During the meeting, the students shared details of their experience and a map of all of the barriers they encountered (including benches in front of lockers that prevented access, and the presence of only one wheelchair-accessible bathroom in the school). The students proposed several locations to install accessibility buttons to improve mobility for people with disabilities. The students' experience was powerful because they had found an authentic audience in the Facilities Director, who acted on their recommendations. The data students provided informed decisions, improving accessibility of the school's buildings.

Global Change Projects

Community-service committees and parents can often provide leads on meaningful community organizations with which to connect. Social entrepreneurs Craig and Marc Kielburger personally take action and encourage other young people to do so through their We Act program. More than 8,000 schools participate in identifying local and global issues, researching issues they are passionate about,

Students wrote banners to explain the benefit of taking action after learning about the many ways students might choose to take action.

Action means anyone can change the world!

and creating plans to take action. (Some We Act actions include bringing in cans of food for the We Scare Hunger food drive, and taking a vow of silence for a day to raise awareness for students whose voices are not heard.) At our school, students suggest initiatives to the school action committee. This committee then helps to promote and run events. As well, many organizations engaged in action are short-staffed and are grateful when students can contribute to their work in real ways.

Assessment and Reflection Ideas

Change projects can provide holistic summative assessment, because many different skill sets must converge for a change project to succeed. Often, research, thinking, self-management, communication, and learning-how-to-learn skills can be assessed through such work.

At the end of a unit, teachers assess the depth of student understanding and skill mastery. There are a number of ways to make summative assessments out of change projects, including assessing written or digital reflections or performances such as debates and movies. Experts who know the subject matter and have a base of conceptual understanding can also be enlisted to evaluate student work. This allows students to feel more invested in the process, because their work is being seen and heard by experts. For example, grade 6 and 7 students spent six weeks preparing a debate to determine if digital devices negatively affect our relationships with family and friends. The judges included a debating expert, a student, and the department head of technology and learning innovation from a neighbouring school, all

stakeholders in the issue. The students were excited to present their arguments and refutations in front of a panel of experts. Students experienced a real sense of significance, as the subject had real-life implications. Because legitimate judges would hear the students' perspectives, there was a buzz and excitement around the debate, and students made sure to thank the experts for their time. Students also learned that we grade

Students participated in a debate with judges who were stakeholders in the debate resolution.

what we value. The debate provided the classroom teacher with grades on research and communication skills.

WHAT IT LOOKS LIKE IN THE CLASSROOM – THE OCEAN MUSICAL IN GRADE 2

The Ocean Musical described below was a major six-week project undertaken by an entire grade. Several teachers and experts designed and facilitated the process and assessed the many written, oral, and performance elements throughout the project.

Creating a musical with grade 2 students required major collaborative skills. Branksome Hall music teacher Luanne Schlueter, and the classroom teachers Christine Bodt and Kendle Sohier, with the help of composer Dean Burry, assisted the students from planning to performing to exploring the central idea: engaging with the arts creates opportunities for self-expression. Although the musical performance idea originated with the music teacher, the classroom teachers also saw the project as a vehicle to share learning with different communities in the school.

To begin the process, students were asked to reflect on their past three units of inquiry to determine the content they wanted to feature in their musical. They chose the ocean habitat as the focus. The music teacher used the students' knowledge about the subject to create a musical, a genre she thought the class would benefit from learning due to its novelty and musicality. To familiarize students with the genre, she arranged field trips to a local children's theatre company and a high-school musical production. Both events exposed students to the many elements of performance, ranging from the playbill to the costumes, songs, and staging. Explicit lessons about the various components of the musical genre filled in the gaps in understanding for the students.

To develop the songs for the show, the teachers brought in an outside expert with knowledge of composition and song writing. With the guidance of the composer, students learned about different building blocks of songs,

Students used their knowledge of ocean habitats to write and perform a musical about ways to protect the oceans.

including rhyming couplets and puns, as background information to build their own songs for their show. The musical did not have a narrator, so students had to use dialogue and songs to communicate key ideas. Using their knowledge of ocean habitats, students worked together with the composer to write songs based on that theme. After songs were created as the spine of the story, the classroom teachers used writer's-workshop time for students to write a script to fill in the remainder of the plot. Other scripts were shared with the students as models. The students also created a playbill to share with the audience on performance days, writing biographical sketches for each actor – a great way to practise paragraph-writing skills. They spent two classes with art teacher Jazz Roy to create the costumes and design the set. Students were extremely excited that a real audience was going to watch the performance they had created note by note. Through the culminating performance in this unit, the students educated and informed a number of audiences about marine stewardship.

After the performance, teachers reflected on the process. They considered adding roles like lighting designer, co-director, and stage manager, to expand on the writer/performer model used in the first year. These different roles would let other students shine through more technical jobs. As well, this approach would provide a more realistic view of the different jobs and responsibilities required to mount a theatrical production. Although additional responsibilities can add more depth to an already rich inquiry, we always need to think about the increased management challenges associated with the coordination of multiple roles and responsibilities.

OH SNAP! *Nothing is ever finished; always reflecting and revising*

Finding an authentic audience who would benefit from knowing about student work can be challenging, but it is worthwhile. One way to find audiences is through parent and community organizations. When students have a real audience, they often take greater care with the accuracy of details and presentation of their work.

It has become easier for students to share their work with the world at large. Tools such as blogs and wikis or photo and video sharing sites allow students to post their work for the world to see. Access to the world afforded by multiple devices opens up the possibility for feedback and discussion with others. Sometimes the classroom itself can offer an authentic audience. Students can consolidate their learning by developing online games or video tutorials to help their peers understand or review concepts. For example, a grade 4 student with strong math skills enjoyed working through challenging math problems. His teacher suggested that he share his solutions and proofs with his peers. He spent much time polishing his work so it could be posted to YouTube for a wider audience.

9 / SUPPORTING CLASSROOM TEACHERS – THE ROLE OF THE ADMINISTRATOR

What It Is

As more is discovered about the human brain and as technology develops, we realize learning is ongoing. Teaching itself can be considered an act of inquiry, as educators strive to understand issues in their schools and classrooms, and take action to make a difference in their lives or the lives of others. Effective administrators provide leadership to facilitate teacher collaboration to plan and teach through inquiry. Strong administrators support teachers as they navigate curriculum content, develop pedagogical strategies, and learn new technologies through job-embedded professional development. Not only are classrooms communities of learning, but the entire school can endorse and embrace ongoing learning as a practice for inquiry to flourish. This chapter is directed to administrators.

Why It Is Important for Inquiry

For inquiry to thrive in the classroom, administrators need to endorse inquiry over and over again through words and actions. They need to model asking questions, maintaining a growth mindset, and, most important, learning from mistakes. With these attitudes and strategies in place, teachers will be better equipped to inquire into their own professional practices. Leaders need to be on board for a school to be bold: championing a coherent approach to developing school curriculum and instruction, and designing and executing a vision for school-wide professional development that includes the creation of professional learning networks.

Vision

What does this process look like? Administrators plan meetings with time for colleagues to collaborate and reflect on teaching and learning. They plan professional development to enhance teacher knowledge about concept-based learning, design provocations, and linking action to student learning. Bold School administrators find ways to celebrate the teaching and learning occurring in classrooms. This can be as simple as a Post-it Note of positive feedback or as grand as an end-of-term breakfast to celebrate student achievements.

Administrators should also spend time gathering firsthand information on what teaching and learning looks like in their schools. In speaking directly with students, they can glean insights into what students value about their learning.

Challenge

Administrators need to manage the many demands inherent in schools. Finding through lines and connection points to manage the work can be challenging.

What Steps Can Administrators Take to Support Teachers?

Empathize and acknowledge the challenges of teaching. Keep an open mind during classroom visits. When you first walk into the classroom, it may not be clear which part of the curriculum the students are tackling. Have conversations with students to see if they are clear on their learning goals, despite how messy the learning might appear. Often, a teacher worries that there might be a problem when an administrator walks in, observes, says nothing, and leaves. Making it clear you will follow up on walk-in visits with formative feedback can set minds at ease.

Incredible morning!

October 20, 2015 at 8:24 AM

All Mail

Folks,

Not only do we wake up to the election being over, and a Jays win, it is also a focus day!!!

We will meet in   as Prep Faculty. Following that we will break into our PLN groups.

So... Just a reminder to identify interest on the chart prior to the meeting this afternoon.
For your convenience, you can access the document here.

Locations for meetings will be identified on the chart. These will be starting places. There may be smaller groups that form (sub-groups) and will find another location.

Reminders re: criteria for the PLN

- job embedded
- connected to a goal
- will develop an action plan (what will you do?)
- assessing effectiveness of PLN for improving student achievement
- when will the next check-in be?

By end of the session today, you should start to sketch out what you want to learn more about and how you are going to move forward. It is probably a good idea to think about what social networks you want to connect to to expand connections beyond   .

This resources might be helpful for guidelines and criteria:
http://www.edutopia.org/blog/how-do-i-get-a-pln-tom-whitby

Please end your session by 3:45pm, as we are all expected in the US Student Centre for a 4pm sharp start, for the GLI presentations.

Happy focus day!

Administrators provide time and map out a process for teachers to collaboratively explore areas of interest and develop professional-learning networks.

Thanks

September 2, 2015 at 9:08 PM
All Mail

Thanks to all of you who participated so fully in the tech expo this afternoon. It has been a very busy 3 days and with the hot afternoon, it was very difficult to stay focused. Thanks especially to our presenters and discussion leaders from the Prep - many of you were nagged by me or Lara during the summer and we so appreciate the time and effort you put into preparing for today.

I saw so many great things happening...

- Sharing experiences
- Sharing failures
- Trying new things
- Helping each other
- Walking out when the session didn't fit and finding something that did
- Asking questions... not just about the technology, but about effective and inspired teaching
- and so much more

We didn't have time to properly gather any feedback at the end of the day, but when you have a moment, we'd appreciate feedback in one of 3 ways:

- tweet a comment or two about today using #UCCtechexpo
- add your "Aha" moment to the Haiku discussion
- if something in particular inspired you, add it to Poll Everywhere (it's working now)

I hope everyone got something useful out of today. Please let me or Lara know how we can help you move forward with anything that might have sparked some interest.

A tech expo organized at the beginning of the school year is a great way for teachers to learn from and with each other.

Classroom Renewal Team

October 24, 2015 at 1:19 PM

Folks,

Classroom renewal process was discussed briefly at 2 meetings in September. There are a few factors which come together such as budgeting timelines and work window opportunities, and so in anticipation of changes to come, it would be prudent to establish some standards for future classroom renewals.

To this end, I'd like to strike a 'Primary Classroom Renewal Team'.

This team would work to pull together the leading thoughts about classroom design for the future, suitable to our context. The deliverable will be **recommendations on what SK-5 classrooms should look like in the future**, to be brought to me prior to the March Break.

I hope you seriously consider this opportunity to think big! You are welcome to come and chat about it if you have any questions.

Please indicate your interest by reply to this email, no later than Halloween.

Many thanks,

Long-term planning committees made up of teachers and administrators can help shape decisions about classroom renovations.

Subject: teacher innovation grant from Character Lab
To: Alice

Hi there! How are you doing? Crazy idea...should we put in a research proposal about creating a culture where making mistakes are valued, expressing gratitude for our mistakes?!

What do you think about a joint project?

https://characterlab.org/teacher-innovation-grant

Hope you are well,

Joint research with another school on determining the value of making mistakes is one way to move school programs and culture forward.

Embrace a Growth Mindset

Celebrate learning journeys. Find opportunities to provide specific and descriptive feedback to teachers on work that is going well. In a culture when many of us rush from project to project, we need to pause to celebrate the process, not just the end products and academic outcomes.

Make failure an accepted part of the learning process. Teachers have a very public job. They are evaluated (however informally) on a daily basis by students, parents, the general public, and even media. They may also be evaluated by peers and administrators. Administrators are encouraged to share and model how they take risks and change their mind based on new learning. For example, at our school we used to write three report cards and have one parent-teacher conference throughout the school year. We realized students were not a central part of this process and, as a faculty, implemented student-led conferences where students could share their learning with their parents. A few years later, after seeing the value of these conferences, we felt there was still too great an emphasis on written reports and not enough on these conversations. After discussing options, teachers proposed only two report cards, replacing the second report card with a three-way conference, with the student, parent, and teacher each playing an equal role. Administrators were open to the change.

Plan for Job-Embedded Professional Development

Create learning opportunities. Support professional development that allows for discussion about pedagogy, content, and technology to meet curriculum guidelines. Our school organizes a technology expo for teachers to present workshops about different learning skills and technological innovations. By working together, teachers stay up-to-date on technological changes and determine how strategies can be harnessed to improve teaching and learning. Other schools set up time for professional learning networks in which teachers can discuss educational areas of interest. For example, a group of teachers (the school counsellor, two classroom teachers, and the learning-strategies teacher) wanted to investigate the benefit of teaching mindfulness for their students to increase their self-regulation skills. The group of four arranged a meeting time to organize a field trip to another school known for its mindfulness program to gain a better sense of how to implement the program. Receiving time from administrators to gather this data facilitated the launch of a similar initiative in their school.

Plan for collaboration and reflection. It is important to find time for collaboration and reflection when teachers are not exhausted or swamped with other work. Limit the time spent in faculty meetings to disseminate information, so more time can be used for collaboration. Every school has its own challenges finding such time, but it is vital to do so if inquiry is going to be effective throughout the school. These meetings don't need the administrator to chair or even to be present. However, as many teachers as possible who work with a particular group of students (i.e., the music teacher, physical education teacher, and so on) should attend. Planning for inquiry-based teaching doesn't need time to create step-by-step lessons but to allow all teachers of a given class to get on the same page about the concepts they wish to teach. Some schools provide time for different teachers to meet during student assemblies; others organize late starts or early dismissals, so teachers can meet with one another.

In addition, teachers should be able to touch base throughout a particular unit so they can assess and reflect on student understanding and determine if they need to take their teaching in a new direction. At the end of a unit of study, teachers also need to regroup to reflect on the unit as a whole, record ideas for the following year, and plan for impact on upcoming units.

Value informal planning time. Finding blocks of time to plan with busy teachers from different departments is an ongoing issue in schools. However, finding dedicated planning time is worthwhile, as, together, teachers can develop interdisciplinary units of inquiry. We also need to acknowledge the informal systems we have in place to overcome time pressures. Classroom teachers often remark on how much planning can be accomplished through hallway and lunchroom conversations. Relationships with colleagues, cultivated over time, make working with each other easier.

Assessment and Reflection Ideas

Informal chats with your faculty will help administrators sense the temperature of the workplace. Surveys taken at the beginning and the end of the school year can provide both qualitative and quantitative data on how faculty feel about school culture, professional development, and collaboration efforts. Getting feedback from teachers and planning to meet their needs models the inquiry-based process teachers use in the classroom.

Teachers participating in professional development should be encouraged to share their learning. When implementing new strategies in their classes, teachers can gather data to determine their effectiveness on student learning. It is heartening when administrators value the research teachers do in their own classrooms and use this learning to inform a school's action plan.

OH SNAP! *Nothing is ever finished; always reflecting and revising*

Administrators need exceptional planning skills to chart a vision that includes long-term support for inquiry, including professional development. One way to do this is to form a planning committee of interested teachers to meet regularly to plan long-term, job-embedded professional development.

Teaching is both a science and an art. Consequently, teachers tend to second-guess themselves. Whenever possible, administrators should endorse and empower teachers.

CONCLUSION – LETTING GO!

Ultimately, we want our students to always feel they are leading lives of significance (Cox 2011). We want students to experience how academic skills are used in the real world. We want them to develop their critical thinking, empathy, and learning-how-to-learn skills to use for the rest of their lives – not just for a test. Students need to know they can make a difference as part of a local and a global community. For us, the most powerful and thought-provoking learning has come from experiences. We want to create similar immersive, open-ended experiences for students that are rooted in empathy and grounded in real issues.

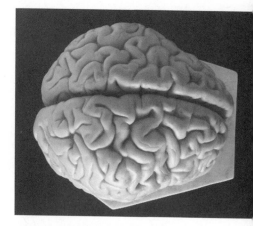

Engaging brains in different types of thinking underpins the work of Bold Schools.

Teaching and learning through inquiry allows teachers to create classroom environments where students engage their brains and feel free to ask their own questions about a topic. While teachers and curriculum documents may determine the destination, learners should play a large role in determining how to get there. This work is messy and requires educators to be lifelong inquirers. Let go of elements of traditional schooling that are no longer appropriate in this age of information, and incorporate what we now know about how we learn to create a Bold School.

Summary: Elements of a Bold School

Collaborate with colleagues. One teacher does not own all the learning for a group of students. Make use of all the adults in the building during high-need times that require more people power, like during the issue-understanding, questioning, research, and editing processes of projects. This approach amplifies the level of support you can provide to help students work on meaningful projects and provide individual attention. The benefit? Students get personalized attention, more consistent feedback, and a small-group environment in which to practise certain skills. Silos need to be removed for real collaboration to occur. Teachers need to evolve from a spirit of cooperation to one of collaboration to realize common goals and ideas.

Let go of timetable restrictions. Sometimes, following student questions will push you in unexpected directions that will take more time. Give yourself and your students permission to explore, to wander, and to take the time to do it. Time should be spent uncovering instead of covering the curriculum. Use professional judgment, and take time when it is needed.

Focus on teaching through concepts. Focus on learning goals, and make big ideas the core of your curriculum. For students to learn about sustainability, humility, conflict resolution, and digital citizenship, for example, plan learning experiences to teach those big ideas. Figure out what experiences need to be planned and what questions need to be asked to get them started on the journey.

Give yourself permission to fail. Brain research confirms we make the most strides when we learn from our mistakes. Celebrate mistakes as learning experiences.

Be present. At the end of the day, kids want to spend time with adults who are curious and who value their love of learning. Create classroom environments where kids feel safe to learn.

Embrace the idea that students can take control of their learning. Learn alongside them. Use technology to meet your learning goals and to connect student work to larger audiences.

Never stop learning. For students to feel like true inquirers, they need to see their teachers wearing the mantle of inquiry with pride. Ask questions, ponder research, take risks, and posit theories alongside your students, and they will become advocates of their own learning.

These ideas are not new. Scholars dating back to Aristotle have supported this approach to education. Creating a Bold School requires real problems to investigate, and audiences to connect with and listen. Embrace the journey of inquiry that can lead to unexpected yet joyful destinations.

STUDENT RESOURCES

Capstone. "PebbleGo: The Emergent Reader Research Solution" (online databases). https://www.pebblego.com/login/index.html.

Deak, . JoAnn. *Your Fantastic Elastic Brain: Stretch It, Shape It.* San Francisco: Little Pickle Press, 2010.

Kahoot! Game-Based Digital Learning Platform. https://getkaho ot.com/.

Kelsey, Elin, and Soyeon Kim. *You Are Stardust.* Toronto: Owlkids Books, 2012.

Little Pickle Press. "Your Fantastic Elastic Brain" (app). http://www.littlepicklepress.com/product/apps/.

Magoon, Scott. *Breathe.* New York: Simon & Schuster/Paula Wiseman Books, 2014.

Marlowe, Sara. *No Ordinary Apple: A Story about Eating Mindfully.* Somerville, MA: Wisdom Publications, 2013.

McCloud, Carol. *Have You Filled a Bucket Today? A Guide to Daily Happiness for Kids.* Boston: Nelson, 2006.

Pirate Pad. "Piratepad." http://piratepad.net.

Prelutsky, Jack. *It's Raining Pigs & Noodles.* New York: Scholastic, 2001.

Red Jumper Book Creator. "The Simple Way to Create Beautiful Books on Your Tablet" (app). http://www.redjumper.net/bookcreator/.

Sesame Street. "Janelle Monae - Power of Yet" (video). YouTube. http://www.youtube.com/watch?v=XLeUvZvuvAs.

Silverstein, Shel. *Where the Sidewalk Ends: The Poems and Drawings of Shel Silverstein.* 25th ed. New York: HarperCollins Publishers, 2000.

Smith, Alexander McCall. *Akimbo and the Elephants.* London: Egmont Books, 2005.

_____. *Akimbo and the Lions.* London: Egmont, 2005.

_____. *Akimbo and the Snakes.* Toronto: Knopf Canada, 2006.

Socrative Inc. "Socrative Teacher" (app). http://www.socrative.com/apps.php.

The Hawn Foundation. *The MindUp Curriculum, Grades 3–5: Brain-Focused Strategies for Learning – and Living.* New York: Scholastic Teaching Resources, 2011.

Vark: A Guide to Learning Styles. "The VARK Questionnaire." http://vark-learn.com/the-vark-questionnaire/.

Via Institute on Character. "The Via Survey: Take Off and Get to Know Your Character Strengths" (online survey). http://www.viacharacter.org/www/The-Survey.

BIBLIOGRAPHY

The Art of Learning. "Welcome to the Art of Learning." Accessed 25 January 2016. http://www.taolearn.com/.

Ban the Bag Brigade. "Home of the Ban the Bag Brigade." Accessed 30 May 2015. https://banthebagbrigade.wikispaces.com/Home.

Bennett, Barrie, and Carol Rolheiser. *Beyond Monet: The Artful Science of Instructional Integration.* Toronto: Barrie Bennett, 2001.

Bennett, Barrie, Carol Rolheiser, and Laurie Stevahn. *Cooperative Learning: Where Heart Meets Mind; An Interactive Resource Book.* Toronto: Educational Connections, 1991.

Black, Paul, and Dylan William. *Inside the Black Box: Raising Standards through Classroom Assessment.* Vol. 1, Pt. 12. London: Dept. of Education & Professional Studies, King's College London, 2005.

Brown, Brené. "Brené Brown: The Power of Vulnerability." Ted Talks (video). Accessed 2 June 2015. https://www.ted.com/talks/brene_brown_on_vulnerability?language=en.

Bucci, Amy. "Explorer of the Week: Mike Wesch." *National Geographic* website. Accessed 30 May 2015. http://voices.nationalgeographic.com/2012/11/19/explorer-of-the-week-mike-wesch/.

Buckley, Don. "Design Thinking – a Year of Innovation." Don Buckley (blog). Accessed 29 May 2012. https://donbuckleyblog.wordpress.com/2012/05/29/design-thinking-a-year-of-innovation/.

Burgess, Teri. "Engaging Students in Sustainable Action Projects (ESSAP) Workshop." Learning for a Sustainable Future. Accessed June 3, 2015. http://resources4rethinking.ca/media/ESSAP%20Guide%20Jan%202009%20-%20FLOW.pdf. 2003

Cecil, Nancy Lee, and Jeanne Pfeifer. *The Art of Inquiry: Questioning Strategies for K–6 Classrooms.* 2nd ed. Winnipeg: Portage & Main Press, 2011.

Chiarotto, Lorraine. *Natural Curiosity: A Resource for Teachers: Building Children's Understanding of the World through Environmental Inquiry.* Toronto: The Laboratory School at the Dr. Eric Jackman Institute of Child Study, Ontario Institute for Studies in Education, University of Toronto, 2011.

Chisholm, Ian, Bradley Chisholm, and Mark Bell. "Coach vs. Mentor." *Developing Leaders.* IEDP, 3, Winter 2011, 14–16.

Cooper, Damian, Karen Adams, and Grant Wiggins. *Talk about Assessment: Strategies and Tools to Improve Learning.* Toronto: Nelson, 2006.

Cox, Adam J. *No Mind Left Behind: Understanding and Fostering Executive Control – The Eight Essential Brain Skills Every Child Needs to Thrive.* New York: TarcherPerigee, 2008.

_____. *Locating Significance in the Lives of Boys.* n.p.: International Boy's School Coalition, 2011. http://www.theibsc.org/page.cfm?p=1698&pback=1678.

Csikszentmihalyi, Mihaly. *Flow: The Psychology of Optimal Experience.* New York: Harper & Row, 1990.

Culin, Katherine R. Von, Eli Tsukayama, and Angela L. Duckworth. "Unpacking Grit: Motivational Correlates of Perseverance and Passion for Long-Term Goals." *The Journal of Positive Psychology* 9, no. 4 (2014): 306–12. doi:10.1080/17439760.2014.898320.

Davidson, Cathy, Howard Rheingold, et al. "Unit 5 - Class #3: Successful Co-Learning Models." (Online panel discussion/video). Connected Courses. 31 October 2014. http://connectedcourses.net/event/unit-5-class-3-successful-co-learning-models/.

Davies, Anne. *Making Classroom Assessment Work.* Merville, B.C.: Connections Pub., 2000.

The Deak Group. "JoAnn Deak, PhD." Accessed 2 June 2015. http://www.deakgroup.com/our-educators/joann-deak-phd/.

Deak, JoAnn, and Terrence Deak. *The Owner's Manual for Driving Your Adolescent Brain*. San Francisco: Little Pickle Press, 2013.

Dillon, Jim T. "Questioning in Education." In *Questions and Questioning*, edited by Michel Meyer. Berlin: Walter de Gruyter & Co., 1988. doi:10.1515/9783110864205.98.

DuckDuckGo. "About DuckDuckGo." Accessed 30 May 2015. https://duckduckgo.com/about.

Dweck, Carol S. *Mindset: The New Psychology of Success*. New York: Random House, 2008.

_____. "Motivate Students to Grow Their Minds." Mindset Works. Accessed 2 June 2015. http://www.mindsetworks.com/.

Erickson, H. Lynn. *Concept-Based Curriculum and Instruction for the Thinking Classroom*. Thousand Oaks, CA: Corwin Press, 2006.

Evans, John, and Eric Jensen. *Teaching with the Brain in Mind*. Alexandria, VA: Association for Supervision and Curriculum Development, 1998.

Flipped Learning Network. "Definition of Flipped Learning." Accessed 12 March 2014. http://flippedlearning.org/domain/46.

Fullan, Michael. *Stratosphere: Integrating Technology, Pedagogy, and Change Knowledge*. Don Mills, ON: Pearson, 2012.

Gardner, Howard. *Frames of Mind: The Theory of Multiple Intelligences*, 3rd ed. New York: Basic Books, 2011.

Gibbs, Jeanne. *Tribes: A New Way of Learning and Being Together*, 4th ed. Santa Rosa, CA: Center Source Publications, 1994.

Google for Education. "Google Apps for Education: A Suite of Free Productivity Tools for Classroom Collaboration." Accessed 3 June 2015. https://www.google.com/edu/products/productivity-tools/.

Google Search Help. "How to Search on Google." Accessed January 25, 2016. https://support.google.com/websearch/answer/134479?hl=en.

Guskey, Thomas R. "The Rest of the Story." *Educational Leadership* 65 (December 2007).

Harvey, Stephanie, and Harvey Daniels. *Comprehension & Collaboration: Inquiry Circles in Action*. Portsmouth, NH: Heinemann, 2009.

Inspiration Software. "Inspire Data: The Visual Way to Explore and Understand Data." Accessed 3 June 2015. http://www.inspiration.com/InspireData.

Institute for the Future. "Future of Learning." Accessed 2 June 2015. http://www.iftf.org/iftf-you/programs-initiatives/future-of-learning/.

International Baccalaureate. "Extended Essay." Accessed 30 May 2015. http://www.ibo.org/en/programmes/diploma-programme/curriculum/extended-essay/.

King, Lance G. *The Importance of Failing Well*. (Master's thesis, University of Waikato, 2009.)

Kozak, Stan, and Susan Elliott. *Connecting the Dots: Key Strategies That Transform Learning for Environmental Education, Citizenship and Sustainability*. North York, ON: Learning for a Sustainable Future, 2014. Online PDF: http://www.lsf-lst.ca/media/LSF_Connecting_the_Dots_full_EN_web.pdf

Louv, Richard. *Last Child in the Woods: Saving Our Children from Nature-Deficit Disorder*. Chapel Hill, NC: Algonquin Books, 2008.

Maiers, Angela. "TEDxDesMoines – Angela Maiers – 'You Matter'." TEDxTalks (video). Accessed 30 May 2015. http://tedxtalks.ted.com/video/TEDxDesMoines-Angela-Maiers-You.

Martin, Roger L. *The Opposable Mind: Winning through Integrative Thinking*. Boston: Harvard Business Review Press, 2009.

Me to We/Free the Children. "Me to We: Together We Change the World." Accessed 25 January 2016. http://www.metowe.com.

Meikuaya, Wilson, Jackson Ntirkana, and Susan McClelland. *The Last Maasai Warriors: An Autobiography*. Vancouver: Douglas & McIntyre, 2013.

Microsoft BI Team. "Balanced Scorecard Co-Creator Dr. Robert Kaplan's New Ways to Improve Communications and Risk Management." Microsoft Business Intelligence (MSDN Blogs). Accessed 8 February 2011. http://blogs.msdn.com/b/microsoft_business_intelligence1/archive/2011/02/09/balanced-scorecard-co-creator-dr-robert-kaplan-s-new-ways-to-improve-communications-and-risk-management.aspx.

Mishra, Punya, and Matthew J. Koehler. "Technological Pedagogical Content Knowledge: A Framework for Teacher Knowledge." *Teachers College Record* 108, no. 6 (2006): 1017–54. doi:10.1111/j.1467-9620.2006.00684.x.

Morrison, Karin, Mark Church, and Ron Ritchhart. *Making Thinking Visible: How to Promote Engagement, Understanding, and Independence for All Learners.* San Francisco: Jossey-Bass, 2011.

November Learning. "Education Resources for Web Literacy." Accessed 25 January 2016. http://novemberlearning.com/educational-resources-for-educators/information-literacy-resources/.

November, Alan. "Empathy: The 21st Century Skill." In *International Society for Technology in Education*, 2012a.

_____. *Who Owns the Learning? Preparing Students for Success in the Digital Age.* Bloomington, IN: Solution Tree Press, 2012b.

Ontario Ministry of Education. *The Ontario Curriculum: Social Studies, Grades 1 to 6; History and Geography, Grades 7 and 8.* Toronto: Service Ontario, 2013. https://www.edu.gov.on.ca/eng/curriculum/elementary/sshg18curr2013.pdf

Orr, Jen. "Thanks to Gary." Elementary, My Dear, or Far From It (blog). Accessed 9 March 2015. http://jenorr.com/?s=Thanks+to+Gary.

Pariser, Eli. "Eli Pariser: Beware Online 'Filter Bubbles'" Ted Talk (video). Accessed 30 May 2015. http://www.ted.com/talks/eli_pariser_beware_online_filter_bubbles?language=en.

Parker, Diane. *Planning for Inquiry: It's Not an Oxymoron!* Urbana, IL: National Council of Teachers of English, 2007.

Pink, Daniel H. *Drive: The Surprising Truth about What Motivates Us.* Edinburgh: Canongate Books, 2011.

Plut, Dijana. "Lev S. Vygotsky." *Prospects: The Quarterly Review of Comparative Education* XXIV, no. 3/4, 1994.

Prensky, Marc R. *Teaching Digital Natives: Partnering for Real Learning.* Thousand Oaks, CA: Corwin Press, 2010.

Primary Years Program Chat Group. "PYP Chat Archives." Accessed 30 May 2015. http://pypchat.wikispaces.com/PYP+Chat+Archives.

Professional Development: Knowledge Building. "What Is Knowledge Building?" Accessed 30 May 2015. http://ikit.org/professionaldevelopment/what-is-knowledge-building.

Rajzman, Michael, Photographer: Asghar Hussain, Vito Amati, Amy Jeanchaiyaphum, and Wasim Hossain. "The Educator's Guide to the We Act Kit" n.p 2014. http://www.weday.com/files/2014/10/WAK-EducatorsGuide-CA-online.pdf.

Richardson, Will. *Why School? How Education Must Change When Learning and Information Are Everywhere* (e-book). New York: TED Conferences, 2012.

Scardamalia, Marlene, and Carl Bereiter. "Knowledge Building: Theory, Pedagogy, and Technology," ed. by K. Sawyer, 97–118. *The Cambridge Handbook of the Learning Sciences*. New York: Cambridge University Press, 2006. doi:10.1017/cbo9780511816833.008.

Seligman, Martin E.P. *Flourish: A Visionary New Understanding of Happiness and Well-Being*. New York: Simon & Schuster Adult Publishing Group, 2011.

Sethi, Kiran. "Kiran Sethi: Kids, Take Charge." Ted Talks (video). Accessed 30 May 2015. https://www.ted.com/talks/kiran_bir_sethi_teaches_kids_to_take_charge?language=en.

Sherratt, Sam. "Help Them Be in Awe Before Asking Them to Care." Time Space Education (blog). Accessed 2 November 2013. https://timespaceeducation.wordpress.com/2013/11/02/help-them-be-in-awe-before-asking-them-to-care/.

_____. "The Power of Simple Provocation." Inquire Within (blog), Accessed 11 July 2013. https://inquiryblog.wordpress.com/2013/07/11/the-power-of-simple-provocation/.

Siegel, Daniel J. *Brainstorm: The Power and Purpose of the Teenage Brain*. New York: TarcherPerigee , 2014.

_____. *Mindsight: The New Science of Personal Transformation*. New York: Bantam, 2010.

Sparking Life: Power Your Brain Through Exercise. "Worldwide Studies and Science Support Exercise or Relieving Symptoms Related to ADD, OCD, Anxiety, Depression, Addiction and Aging." Accessed 21 February 2016. http://sparkinglife.org/page/why-exercise-works.

Stanford University Institute of Design. "Welcome to the Virtual Crash Course in Design Thinking." Accessed 30 May 2015. http://dschool.stanford.edu/dgift/.

TPack.org. "TPack Explained." Accessed 4 June 2015. http://tpack.org/.

Via Institute on Character. "The Via Survey: Take Off and Get to Know Your Character Strengths" (online survey). Accessed 18 February 2016. http://www.viacharacter.org/www/The-Survey.

Visible Thinking Project. "Visible Thinking." Accessed 4 June 2015. http://www.visiblethinkingpz.org/VisibleThinking_html_files/VisibleThinking1.html.

Von Culin, Katherine R., Eli Tsukayama, and Angela L. Duckworth. "Unpacking grit: Motivational correlates of perseverance and passion for long-term goals." *The Journal of Positive Psychology*. V.9, No. 4, 2014. http://dx.doi.org/10.1080/17439760.2014.898320.

We Day/Free the Children. "Weaving Service into AP Courses." Accessed 30 April 2015. http://www.weday.com/2015/04/weaving-service-ap-courses/.

Weinberger, David. *Too Big to Know: Rethinking Knowledge Now That the Facts Aren't the Facts, Experts Are Everywhere, and the Smartest Person in the Room Is the Room*. New York: Basic Books, 2012.

Wiggins, Grant P., and Jay McTighe. *Understanding by Design*. Alexandria, VA: Association for Supervision and Curriculum, Development, 1999.

Wilhelm, Jeffrey D. *Engaging Readers & Writers with Inquiry: Promoting Deep Understandings in Language Arts and the Content Areas with Guiding Questions*. New York: Scholastic Teaching Resources, 2007.